An early 3½-liter Bentley from the thirties. The saloon body was by Barker, original owner was the Marquis of Bath. Cars similar to this may be available at bargain prices.

Paul R. Woudenberg

Illustrated
ROLLS-ROYCE
BENTLEY
BUYER'S
GUIDE T.M.

Motorbooks International ®
Publishers & Wholesalers Inc
Osceola, Wisconsin 54020, USA

First published in 1984 by Motorbooks International Publishers & Wholesalers Inc, PO Box 2, 729 Prospect Avenue, Osceola, WI 54020 USA

Printed and bound in the United States of America

The information in this book is true and complete to the best of our knowledge. All recommendations are made without any guarantee on the part of the author or publisher, who also disclaim any liability incurred in connection with the use of this data or specific details

Cover photography by Ted Reich

Library of Congress Cataloging-in-Publication Data
Woudenberg, Paul R.
  Illustrated Rolls-Royce & Bentley buyer's guide.

  Bibliography: p.
  1. Rolls-Royce automobile—History. 2. Bentley automobile—History.
3. Rolls-Royce automobile—Purchasing. 4. Bentley automobile—Purchasing. I. Woudenberg, Paul R. Illustrated Rolls-Royce & Bentley buyer's guide. II. Title. III. Title: Illustrated Rolls-Royce & Bentley buyer's guide.
TL215.R6W68 1987   629.2′222   87-15263
ISBN 0-87938-264-3 (soft)

Acknowledgments

Four readers have supplied many suggestions and helpful criticisms and the author is greatly indebted to them for their time and aid. Dr. Robin O. Barnard in Surrey is the historian of the Twenty-Ghost Club and is a distinguished authority especially in the prewar cars. He owns one of the finest personal motoring libraries of the world. David Preston, Press and Public Relations Manager of Rolls-Royce Motors, Crewe, graciously consented to review the entire manuscript and has helped greatly especially with the postwar period. Richard Barton of London has had long experience in direct contact with the cars, lectures frequently on Rolls-Royce, and is an advisor to the Rolls-Royce Enthusiasts Club. He has abundant professional expertise on repair and restoration. Ted Reich is the former president of the Rolls-Royce Owners Club and is highly regarded for his encyclopedic knowledge of both Rolls-Royce and Bentley.

The author has consulted other experts in the field on particular matters including Stanley Garthwaite, Andrew Spranza, Ivor Gordon, Hugh Keller, Phil Hill, Emery Wanless, David Scott, Sam Shoup, Dennis Miller-Williams, Win Estes, Bob Barrymore and Paul Steward among others.

Pictures have come from several sources. The author is greatly indebted to Frank Dale and Stepsons for the use of many pictures from its superb archives. Dr. Barnard has supplied numerous rare pictures. Ted Reich has been very generous. Owners have consented graciously to allow their cars to be pictured.

Though specifications for Rolls-Royce and Bentley cars are found in many sources, the best job of compiling and updating the basic material is by the Rolls-Royce Owners' Club of America. The contribution of this fine club to the hobby cannot be overstressed. The specifications in this book follow the system developed by the RROC.

My thanks especially go to my wife who has diligently read her way through the manuscript with fruitful results. Her enthusiasm when we buy these motorcars is only equaled by her enthusiasm when we sell.

Rolls-Royce and Bentley history is particularly legend-laden and historians struggle to sift truth from myth. All Divine and editorial help may not save an author from folly and remaining errors are, of course, his responsibility. Suggestions, criticisms and comments are welcome.

Preface to the second edition

Since 1984, Rolls-Royce and Bentley prices have continued to escalate in response to heightened collector demand, auctions and currency shifts. British prices have moved up sharply. Auction records for pre-World War I Ghosts have now exceeded $200,000. The decline of the dollar in 1987 has also lifted the U.S. market in response to European and Japanese buyers. In the light of this changing market, each model in this guide has been reexamined. Some ratings have been changed and additional information has been supplied when appropriate.

The author wishes to thank Ted Reich for proofing and suggestions.

Paul R. Woudenberg
Pebble Beach

Investment Rating

★ A common, readily available model of modest investment potential.

★★ Model which can be found with patience, with good investment potential.

★★★ A car that is hard to find and infrequently offered. Usually has strong investment possibilities. May include models that are "undiscovered" or await a new class of more sophisticated buyers.

★★★★ Rare model of very high collecting value.

★★★★★ Car of exceptional interest, rarity and value.

Rarity and potential appreciation have a close relationship in cars of great merit. The rating values assigned to each model are thus both a measurement of availability and an estimate of potential based on the price performance of the car in the past decade. Some models have appreciated very rapidly in recent years and are somewhat overpriced at the present time; other models may be currently undervalued. Particular comments on current market conditions may be found in the text.

For the newer cars, beginning with the Silver Shadow in 1965, the ratings reflect, in some cases, estimates of potential. Rarity and open coachwork will almost always enhance investment possibility. The uniformity of the Shadow series over a lengthy production run tends to allow these cars to depreciate more in accord with normal used-car market conditions, at least in saloon form. Prices will depend on factors such as mileage, general condition and proven history. In the longest perspective, say thirty years, all Rolls-Royces and Bentleys will have substantial collectible value.

Table of Contents

Introduction

The Best Car in the World?

There have been many great cars created in the past century but none surpass the Rolls-Royce in public recognition. The inspired slogan "The Best Car in the World" is arguable and often disputed but Rolls-Royce has succeeded in fastening this idea to its products.

There are several good reasons for the remarkable eminence of the marque. The quality of the product is undeniable. Engineering has, at times, been conservative if not downright anachronistic. The design of mechanical components is often fussy and unnecessarily complicated, albeit in the interest of refinement. And there have been technical errors from time to time whose residual effects make the buying of certain aged models risky. But no one who has ever worked on these cars faults the exquisite attention to detail and the fidelity of assembly which mark all models.

Another reason for the eminence of the Rolls-Royce is that the company has never built a cheap car. Mercedes, a very worthy challenger, has, over the course of the years, built cars to compete in virtually every part of the market except the very cheapest, and has produced a full line of commercial vehicles. Thus, the "image" of Mercedes has a blurred focus. Rolls-Royce, on the other hand, has always presented under its own badge only one type of car, namely, the most-refined high-quality product possible aimed at the luxury trade. To be sure, the 20 hp car introduced in 1922 was "smaller" and broadened the market for the company, but the price was still very high and the quality no less than the Silver Ghost. It was not a car bought for commercial service.

Furthermore, Rolls-Royce remains the only company from the very early days to have survived in the automobile market through building only a luxury product. Hispano-Suiza, Pierce-Arrow, Delaunay-Belleville and Napier, not to mention a host of other rivals, have all gone; yet Rolls-Royce continues to provide the same sort of automobile in the same relative price class that it did in 1910. This is an astonishing achievement and contributes to the peculiarities of the Rolls-Royce marketplace.

Unlike the "dead" cars of the past, now so eagerly sought after by collectors, the Rolls-Royce remains a living legend. This creates a novel market problem. The owner of a new Silver Spur may have little marque enthusiasm in common with the collector tenderly caring for his Silver Ghost. At some point in between, however, the Rolls-Royce ceases to be mere ostentatious transport and becomes an object of veneration. At that point the measurement of a car's value subtly shifts. Is a 1957 Silver Cloud to be owned as refined transportation or has it become essentially a "collector car"?

The motives of Rolls-Royce buyers are varied. Since the car is so well known, it has become a favorite of both "image buyers" and speculators. These buyers are often untutored and make assumptions of value and potential from their own inner visions. Likewise, their representation of a car when they sell it may have little relationship to the facts. Such commerce muddies the marketplace for genuine collectors and restorers.

The problem became more acute in the past decade since the cost of a new Rolls-Royce rose tremendously, requiring a substantial financial standing to enter the market. Wealthy buyers may not always have the time nor inclination to pursue the true state of the market at any given moment. Faced with the daunting prospect of an investment of nearly a hundred thousand dollars for a Silver Spirit, they may find a secondhand example of the Silver Shadow, for example, an attractive proposition at a price which, in comparison to the new cars, seems a bargain. In truth, the secondhand price may be wildly inflated. Such sales, and they are not infrequent, tend to further skew the market and make appraisal more difficult.

Recent Market Trends

The price of the Silver Shadow has risen rapidly since the late sixties. This has had the effect of supporting prices of the used Shadow market and sometimes causing real appreciation. It has had the further effect of firming prices on most of the postwar Rolls-Royce and Bentley automobiles, at least those which are in the normal marketplace. The prewar cars in the hands of collectors have not kept pace and, though they have rapidly appreciated, very few models can command the cost of a new Corniche, which is now $173,800. We are thus confronted with the unusual situation of the current product selling for more than the greatest collectibles in the history of the company, with very few exceptions, among them the pre-1914 Ghosts.

The Rolls-Royce market, therefore, offers a wide variety of choices to the buyer. Given a fixed amount of money, say $100,000, one can buy a Rolls-Royce of virtually any vintage. With some good research, the figure could be lowered to $50,000 (with limitations). There is no other automobile that has such a uniformity of value over its entire production span and this fact contributes to the public's extraordinary fascination with the Rolls-Royce.

The Bentley market is quite different and should be divided into three periods. The vintage Bentley, from 1922 to 1931, was produced by the original independent company in Cricklewood, London, headed by W. O. Bentley. The models this firm produced were very different from the contemporary Rolls-Royce motorcars. Collectors of these vintage Bentleys form a tightly knit cult.

The second period, from 1933 to 1940, is another specialized era of somewhat lesser stature. These Bentleys were built in Derby by Rolls-Royce; and though there was a similarity of design philosophy and detailing, the Bentleys were entirely different—much smaller and quicker than the Rolls-Royces.

The third period begins in 1945 when the Bentley was reintroduced by Rolls-Royce as a mass-produced car featuring attractive standard steel saloon coachwork, though private builders continued to use the chassis. The marque gradually lost identity, particularly when the Silver Dawn began using the same standard steel saloon body in 1949. After 1956 the Rolls-Royce and Bentley were virtually the same car. After 1959 the Rolls-Royce sold in greater volume as customers opted for what they viewed as more prestige at just about the same price. By 1980 the Bentley accounted for less than ten percent of production.

Over the years the Bentley has not enjoyed the same constancy of image as the Rolls-Royce. However, the Bentley offers the collector exceptional treats, even beyond the prewar cars, including the rare and expensive postwar Continentals, the last Bentleys with individuality. Conversely, some of the lowest-priced cars available in the whole Rolls-Royce/Bentley market are the postwar Bentley Mark VI's. Thus, the Bentley models require careful study for the novice and present both tempting bargains and exceptionally high-priced esoterica.

Why Buy a Rolls-Royce or Bentley?

The Rolls-Royce and Bentley remain especially fascinating cars because people answer this question in many different ways. The cachet of the Rolls-Royce remains a strong motivation for new-car buyers. It has continued to fulfill the mystique of being "The Best Car in the World," a marvelous achievement. There are likely better-engineered cars, cars offering equivalent ride, greater performance and perhaps even greater luxury at much lower prices. But the Rolls-Royce continues its hold at the top of the market because of a melange of qualities.

People buy Rolls-Royce motor cars for image building, so necessary in, for example, the movie industry. They buy them for investments, counting on the relentless price increases to hold values at least steady. The older cars are bought by collectors and hobbyists, by speculators and dealers. Some buy them because of the exquisite mechanical details on extraordinary coachwork, so evident in the earlier cars. Some buy them for the associations that might come through clubs and events.

But all Rolls-Royce owners seem to share the satisfaction, for one reason or another, of a pride of ownership which, rightly or wrongly, is rarely equaled among owners of other cars. There are far more exclusive groups of owners, more knowledgeable groups of owners, and groups which use their old cars more vigorously. But the Rolls-Royce retains that indefinable magic that is the sign of the greatest of cars. To have retained this in the face of very broad ownership is remarkable.

Within the Rolls-Royce fraternity, there is a variety of interesting focal points. Postwar cars continue to grow in sheer numbers and constitute by far the largest part of the market. The earlier cars, especially the small-horsepower models from 1922 to 1939, have not kept pace in appreciation because their use and management require a higher level of mechanical skills and the collectors have historically been drawn to the more dramatic big cars of the 40/50 hp series. Even the big cars in the more sedate body styles have been outvalued by the extraordinarily high prices of the new models.

This was not always so. The Rolls-Royce old car movement in America began with a focus on the cars produced in Springfield, Massachusetts, principally the Phantom I. Prices were low and the hobby was small. Through the sixties, cars of virtually any period were readily available at very affordable prices. The increased popularity of auction sales and the publicity that flowed from them awakened many people to the future, beginning with the auction sale of the Sword collection in Scotland in 1962. In Britain, the Silver Ghost and the Twenty became the nucleus of early collecting, because the later prewar cars were still in service. As prices soared and the market exploded, the postwar cars received new attention from collectors. Today the Bentley Drivers Club struggles with formulas to hold the balance between vintage, Derby-built and postwar models. The Rolls-Royce clubs have received all comers. In the Rolls-Royce Owners' Club of the U.S., sixty-one percent of the cars are post-1946.

The large group of postwar owners contains some collectors who constitute a potential buying group for the earlier cars. There is subtle pressure in the clubs and in concours competition to promote this trend. The postwar cars, so often with standard factory coachwork, by their very numbers have a sort of monotony that is accentuated at meets and shows. Only fear of maintenance and breakdown acts against this trend. Therefore, one expects a steady upward pressure on prices for the prewar cars, even those of modest merit.

The postwar group is steadily augmented by new people acquiring the Rolls-Royce cachet, both in new and used forms. This remains the principal reason for the remarkable growth of both the American Rolls-Royce Owners' Club and the British Rolls-Royce Enthusiasts' Club. These clubs are exceptionally active and provide tours, field events, technical information and mechanical support for owners. The Bentley Drivers Club offers parallel support and provides excellent service manuals, reprints and technical studies. This club remains essentially a British-based group, an "old boy" network, where activities are focused more on rallies; American events are widespread and less frequent.

First Steps in Buying a Rolls-Royce or Bentley

Nothing beats knowledge when buying any car. Fortunately, buyers of Rolls-Royce and Bentley automobiles have available a large bibliography supported by excellent club journals and technical reprints. The standard history seems to be *The Rolls-Royce Motor Car* by Anthony Bird and Ian Hallows, first published in 1964. There are many other works which are listed in the annotated bibliography. There is no comparable Bentley history, though Bird and Hallows do treat the post-1933 product. But there are many fine books on Bentley, not the least of which are the several reminiscences by W. O. Bentley himself.

It would be prudent to join the Rolls-Royce Owners' Club in the United States and to secure back issues of the *Flying Lady* (all available), a fine bimonthly magazine which will quickly give much technical and historical information as well as a "feel" of the marketplace through classified ads. The Rolls-Royce Enthusiasts' Club in Britain offers a comparable service and journal. The Bentley Drivers Club is a venerable group of dedicated owners whose *Review* is admirable, albeit more for "insiders." A useful advertisement section accompanies both British journals.

The major U.S. automobile magazines continue to be a good source for Rolls-Royces and Bentleys. The ubiquitous *Hemmings, Old Cars Weekly, Cars & Parts* and similar journals plus regional equivalents such as *West Coast Car Collector* can be helpful. In Britain *Motor Sport, Exchange and Mart* and numerous specialist magazines fill the same function. The more-general auto magazines such as *Road & Track* are limited in part because the Rolls-Royce market is so sharply focused. The Sunday editions of the major newspapers in the metropolitan areas are a fine source of late model Rolls-Royces. The *Los Angeles Times, The New York Times* and *The Wall Street Journal* should routinely be read, both for market indications and possible opportunities. In Britain, the *Sunday Times* has the largest number of used Rolls-Royce advertisements.

Availability

The availability of cars is constantly changing, due to numerous factors. In times of high interest rates, the speculators are flushed out and distress selling can take place. This is especially true of the "image owner" whose pride gives way to necessity. Since the cost of owning a Rolls-Royce or Bentley on a sheer capital basis can be heavy, high interest rates tend to focus enthusiasm and sharpen selectivity.

Death is a factor. The Rolls-Royce Owners' Club was founded in 1951 by mature men. Their precious cars, often owned for decades, appear from time to time. Second-generation buyers often benefit from the dedication of these early founding members. Since the club was founded basically upon the American-built Springfield Rolls-Royce, these cars often are the magnificent Brewster-bodied Phantoms, though as the hobby expanded many fine British cars appeared.

It was fashionable and prudent in the fifties and sixties to go to Britain to buy Rolls-Royces and Bentleys. The prices in England were cheap then and the abundance of cars was dazzling. This advantage has lessened for four reasons.

1. The English market appreciated very rapidly in the seventies, faster than in the U.S. In recent years, car prices were often higher in Britain than in the U.S. However, better exchange rates after 1982 have made the British cars more attractive for U.S. buyers.

2. So many cars were brought to the U.S. that European buyers have often scoured America when exchange rates were favorable. The U.S. availability may be larger than in the British market, at least in some areas.

3. The British climate was hard on the steel-bodied postwar cars and often the rust problems are very serious. This is especially true of the early Mark VI Bentleys, and even the Silver Clouds and Bentley S series seem to have moisture traps everywhere. Many a U.S. buyer has imported a car at a bargain price, quite unprepared to face the massive rebuilding necessary.

4. The U.S. smog and safety regulations have slowed the import of post-1967 cars, which were not built to U.S. specifications.

Some Added Precautions

The identification of a Rolls-Royce is critically important because so many cars are misrepresented. The key is the chassis number, found on a plate on the engine side of the firewall near the hood, or bonnet. It is always easily visible. The car can instantly be dated and the model precisely identified through the chassis number.

Armed with a correct chassis number it is often possible to determine if the body on the car is correct, and if irregularities have taken place. Two of the Dalton Watson Rolls-Royce books, *Coachwork on Rolls-Royce* and *Rolls-Royce: The Elegance Continues*, have useful indexes on various coachbuilders, which can date and validate original coachwork precisely. John Fasal's *The Rolls-Royce Twenty* contains a complete index of all chassis of that model. Ray Gentile's *The Rolls-Royce Phantom II Continental* has a complete index of the Continentals, and a detailed discussion about identifying this splendid model. The prewar Bentley market is well cared for by Stan Sedgwick's *All the Pre-War Bentleys—As New*, with a complete index of

Many early Ghosts ended their days as rugged breakdown trucks. This hardy 1910 veteran, number 1390, was particularly abused. Ghosts are rarely found in this condition anymore and the value would be modest since the reconstruction cost would approach or exceed $100,000. This particular car is now bodied with a splendid Jarvis replica of C. H. Rolls' famous H. J. Mulliner balloon car. Robin Barnard photo.

all chassis, which is critically important because of so many body and engine swaps on the early cars. With these books it is often possible to measure the seller's claims against solid information.

Yet another resource is available for members of the three major clubs. The Rolls-Royce and Bentley motorcars are unusually well documented with factory records. The clubs have chassis cards and make copies available to members for a small fee. Information on some models can be very detailed and helpful.

Some Bentleys and not a few Rolls-Royces have second or third bodies. The chassis were robust and outlasted the coachwork. In the thirties, specialist firms in England rebodied many 20 hp cars in contemporary and stylish modes for resale. Also, there were body swaps by original owners, often close to the time of first purchase.

The problem of replica bodies is exceptionally complex and continues to be heavily debated. Does a car with a second body from the same period have a lesser value? Does a flawless modern replica reduce the value of a car? Here are some guiding principles:

First, a car with a modern replica body often fails to meet esthetic standards and can easily be detected by the absence of compound curves, crude contemporary hardware and generally clumsy design. Most often such bodies are open tourers, which require the lowest level of coachbuilding skill, and are cheap to produce and easy to sell. The cars are often spotted by the mismating of front and rear fenders, the fronts retained from the original body and the rears freshly produced to match the new body. Such cars can be well finished but are of limited value because, although they may be bought and sold well, the buying public tends to become more sophisticated and will eventually make appropriate esthetic judgments. The astute purchaser will probably avoid these cars or perhaps base the price on chassis value alone.

Second, the replica bodies of the thirties, such as those by Southern Motors, are usually very much prettier than some of the modern crudities. In the fifties such replicas were scorned by collectors for three reasons: a) The coachwork was built to a low price in order to sell and was frequently of modest quality. b) The proportions of the car were never quite right, partly because of the larger wheels of the early 20 hp cars. And c) the 20 hp cars were so slow that the fitting of a rakish drophead body was a contradiction too great to be enjoyed. As prices have risen, these particular replicas have found more favor and, within their limits, are pleasant cars.

Third, contemporary flawless replicas, apart from the above-mentioned crudities, present problems to concours judges. Originality is always the most desired goal, yet a decrepit body replaced by a carefully crafted duplicate certainly keeps a car on the road. These questions often appear in the highest-priced markets, such as Duesenberg, where a superb modern recreation of an original racy style can be justified economically. Not a few Bentleys have been rebodied with reproduction Vanden Plas tourers of very high quality. In the case of the vintage Bentley, many early saloons were rebodied with tourers. One wonders about the discarded saloons and other period coachwork which, in the longest view, may come to be regarded as lost treasures. Before accepting the seller's appraisal of his flawless replica, even a precise duplication of an original style, it would be wise to call in all help possible, not only to check authenticity, but to test the esthetic result.

And fourth, it sometimes happened that the original owner of a vintage car disliked the body and would fit another one after a relatively short period of ownership, even a few months. Such exchanges present less trouble because the quality level of the coachwork is generally unchanged. Still, it is probably better to find the original coachwork on the chassis, regardless of all other factors.

The appraisal of a car is both an art and a science and still depends heavily on experience. However, the novice should not forget that the interior of the car gives the quickest clue to general condition. Originality is instantly observable along with general wear. Exterior cosmetics and mechanical matters are not only readily repairable but may be given hurried treatment. However, interiors are exceptionally difficult to reproduce to original standards and the cost is proportionately higher than other restoration problems.

Where to Buy

There are many authorized Rolls-Royce dealers who provide sales and service for postwar cars. Few will work on prewar cars, leaving this market to a substantial group of private specialists. Happily, the Rolls-Royce is well catered to, and owners need not fear being "orphaned." But service costs for a $100,000 automobile will be high. Likewise, the price of parts and service for the older cars reflects their values. In all fairness, the remanufactured critical parts such as cylinder heads, though expensive, are more a tribute to the enthusiasm of the producer rather than to profit. The important thing is that the cars can be kept running.

Dealer trading in the post-1945 Rolls-Royce market is large. It is a truly national market in the United States, with advertisements appearing from all over the country in major newspapers as mentioned earlier. Buyers are expected to personally view the auto, and such costs are often absorbed by the dealer upon sale. The British market is similar, with the concentration of sales in the London area.

Dealer prices will normally be higher to reflect inventory flooring cost, profit and the general costs of business. But private parties can have inflated estimates, which may be higher than a dealer's. Furthermore private sellers often exaggerate descriptions of the cars and may unwittingly pass along bogus claims, histories and stories of prior ownership, which all too often are eagerly grasped by the buyer. There are few cars that so well repay study as a defense against fraud as do Rolls-Royces and Bentleys.

Rolls-Royces and Bentleys appear frequently at auctions and a genuine sale is a good indication of the market value. The hazard of using auction prices for measurement is that the cars are often poorly appraised and tested. A casual observer checking prices may thus get a distorted impression of the market. There is also a possibility that a car may be offered by a seller to test the "temperature" of the market without a true effort to consummate a sale. Needless to say, auction buyers should make strenuous efforts to pretest and drive prospective cars. In Britain it is normal practice to auction cars without any possibility being offered of hearing the engine run. Given the right auction at the right time, bargains can surely be found. It takes a steady nerve, some cautious friends at one's elbow and an unclouded head to buy well at auctions.

Some rust problems for all Clouds and Bentley S series: Dirt collects on the inside lip of the fender cut-out and holds moisture. The fender parking lamps are another trouble spot because the rust protection was compromised when the attachment was made.

CHAPTER 1
INTRODUCTION TO THE PREWAR CARS

The prewar cars have always held a fascination for collectors for two basic reasons. First, Rolls-Royce and Bentley built no standard factory coachwork before 1945—each car is unique. In the thirties, cars were occasionally contracted in batches of about twenty-five units, such as the steel Park Ward saloon on the Bentley 4¼ chassis of which perhaps over 400 were built. Even in this case, the bodies had numerous detail differences from car to car. In general, however, the coachwork of the prewar cars was highly individual, often eccentric, and could reflect the whims of the purchaser. This makes the prewar cars very interesting. It also makes uniform appraisal very difficult. How can one compare a seven-passenger formal limousine with a rakish torpedo tourer built on the same chassis? Thus, a rating of a particular model, say a Phantom I, is but a general guide. Most collectors seek out the lighter, more sporting coachwork, while limousines and sedate saloons have a less enthusiastic following.

Second, the quality and workmanship of the coachbuilt cars before the war was higher than after 1945. Though this may be argued, economics tend to confirm this judgment. Labor costs were extremely low in England and Rolls-Royce did not shrink from elaborate assembly methods requiring the intensive use of skilled labor. This is the reason for the extraordinary detail on these cars. The chassis price of a prewar car ranged from about 1,100 pounds (approximately $5,500) to 1,800 pounds ($9,000) on the small and large cars, respectively. The buyer then had to contract for coachwork. It should be remembered that a 1938 Packard V-12 formal sedan could be bought for under $5,000 in Detroit, built by far more expensive American labor. The Phantom III V-12 Rolls-Royce could well have sold for roughly three times the cost of the competing Packard, even *with* cheap English labor.

By 1949, Rolls-Royce was able to offer the complete Silver Dawn in New York for just under $10,000; although the pound was worth virtually half of the prewar rate, and with much higher labor costs. A coachbuilt Silver Dawn might be $15,000, a Silver Wraith somewhat higher. A Phantom III in 1949 built to 1938 standards would have cost at least $50,000!

What was lost was the exquisite attention to detail, the costly techniques of aluminum crankcases, multiple ignition systems and a host of other useful and often eccentric features of the prewar cars.

*　　*　　*

The early history of the Rolls-Royce is covered by numerous authors, perhaps most comprehensively by C. W. Morton in *A History of Rolls-Royce Motor Cars, 1903-1907* which is now out of print. Before the Silver Ghost, there were approximately 106 cars built by Rolls-Royce in two-, three-, four- or six-cylinder form. Three two-cylinder 10 hp cars survive, as well as one three-cylinder 15 hp car, two four-cylinder 20 hp cars and one six-cylinder 30 hp car. Three V-8's were also built, of which none survive. Of the above remaining cars, institutional ownership accounts for three, while private owners have the remaining four. The availability of any of these early cars for purchase is thus severely limited, and all of them are rated five stars.

The production Rolls-Royces are divided into two main groups: large- and small-horsepower models. The Silver Ghost, rated as a 40/50 horsepower car by the old British tax rating system, was a six-cylinder car of over seven liters displacement. Its successors, the Phantom I, II and III, were also called 40/50's and were in the over-seven-liter category. The Phantom I and II continued the big six-cylinder formula of the Silver Ghost, but the Phantom III was a V-12.

In 1922 the small-horsepower series began with the Twenty, named for the horsepower tax rating, with an engine of just over three liters displacement. The engine and car gradually enlarged, to 3.7 liters in 1929 and 4.257 liters in 1936. The large-horsepower models did not survive the war and the small-engined car became the basis for postwar production.

One of the very rare pre-Silver Ghost Rolls-Royces, in this case the 1905 10 hp, two-cylinder model, number 20165. It is owned by Rolls-Royce Ltd., and is often on display at the London showrooms on Conduit Street. It is the third oldest Rolls-Royce in existence. Rolls-Royce Ltd. photo.

Most specification and serial number data contained in this book is through the generous courtesy and cooperation of the Rolls-Royce Owners Club of America.

EARLY CARS

Approximate number produced: 106, including the 3 Royce cars.

1904	Royce cars 2 cyl.	1905/6	26355 6 cyl. 30 hp. 3 pairs of cylinders
1904/5	20150-20163 2 cyl. 10 hp.		26370-26375
	20165-20167	1906	40500-40511 4 cyl. 20 hp.
1905	23924 3 cyl. 15 hp.		40519-40533
1905	23926 4 cyl. 20 hp.	1906	40518 V-8 "Legalimit"
1905	23927 6 cyl. 30 hp., Scrapped	1906/7	60500-60511 6 cyl. 30 hp. 3 pairs of cylinders
1905	24263/4 4 cyl. 20 hp.		60524-60538
1905	24272/3 3 cyl. 15 hp.	1905	80500 V-8
1905	24274/5 6 cyl. 30 hp. 3 pairs of cylinders		
1905	26330/2 3 cyl. 15 hp.		
1905/6	26350-26354 4 cyl. 20 hp.		
	26356-26359		

15

History

In the summer of 1906, Henry Royce completed the design of a new six-cylinder car to replace the unsatisfactory six-cylinder 30 hp car of which thirty-seven examples had been built. To overcome crankshaft vibration and even breakage, Royce concentrated on the lower end of the engine with a massive new crankshaft set in seven very large main bearings in a very stiff crankcase. Two blocks of three cylinders each had integral heads so that there would be no gasket failures. Compression was a very modest 3.2 to 1 with about 50 bhp developed at only 1500 rpm. The result was an engine of absolute smoothness, quite above anything else of the period.

Royce compounded the triumph with superb electrics, an unusually fine carburetor, full-pressure lubrication and roller cam followers on little arms which have delighted Rolls-Royce fanciers ever since. Early tests and trials established the car's total reliability, silence and flexibility. Top speed was about 50 mph.

The success of the new car, called the Silver Ghost because of the dramatic paint and plating of the thirteenth chassis (still in the possession of the company), caused Rolls-Royce to standardize on one model in March 1908. The young company was under-capitalized which made it imperative that work should be concentrated on the model with the most potential. The engine stroke was lengthened in 1909 to 4¾ inches (7.428 cc displacement). The original four-speed transmission inherited from the 30 hp six-cylinder model, with a geared-up fourth, was changed to three speeds in 1909 and then in 1913 back to four speeds but with a direct top, used initially on the "colonial" type chassis.

The London-Edinburgh special car prepared in 1911 in answer to the rival Napier's claims brought an increase in compression to 3.5 and a larger carburetor which raised horsepower to fifty-eight. The torque tube drive and cantilever springs used on the special car were fitted to all chassis from number 2100 until the close of production. By 1914, the reputation of the Silver Ghost was well on the way to justifying the claim "The Best Car in the World." The open, lightly bodied Silver Ghosts prepared for the 1913 Austrian trial had a maximum speed of over 80 mph.

The Silver Ghost remained in limited production for war use through 1917, some chassis being fitted with armored coachwork for use in the Middle East while others, including many pre-1914 chassis, were used as staff cars and ambulances. Production for private sales resumed in 1919, the Ghost now fitted with a chain-driven self-starter mounted beside the transmission. Horsepower was about seventy at around 2200 rpm. Four-wheel brakes with an excellent mechanical servo system appeared very late in the S series and were retrofitted at substantial factory cost on EM and LM chassis after a premature announcement in October 1923 forced the company to guarantee installation on two-wheel-braked cars already released. Autovac fuel feed replaced the pressure system in 1924. Production ceased in 1925.

Identification

The pre-1914 Silver Ghost is externally identified by parallel hood sides, though tapering appears with some of the sporting coachwork following the London-Edinburgh model of 1911. The early cars had lower radiators, wooden wheels and, often, bell-shaped headlamps. Collectors of pre-1914 Ghosts are generally very well versed on the many particulars of model identification; since authenticity is critical in the early cars, any buyer is well advised to seek expert help to ensure originality. The later Ghosts, after 1919, were almost always fitted with wire wheels. The cantilever rear springs were often exposed above the running boards. Late Ghosts, however, are not always easily distinguished externally from early Phantom I's.

Several coachbuilders erected London-Edinburgh-style tourers on the prewar Ghosts. This splendid, genuine example on a 1913 chassis is by Holmes of Derby. It should command a top price, at least in the $100,000 range. Robin Barnard photo.

This 1914 Barker tourer, 36MA, is an exquisite design highlighted by the splendid cape hood. Price should be high. Robin Barnard photo.

As is always the case with Rolls-Royce cars, check the serial number on the aluminum plate on the firewall for precise identification.

Performance and Utility

The Silver Ghost is a very reliable car and may be driven virtually anywhere with confidence. The pre-1919 cars must be hand cranked, not an insignificant job with a 7.4-liter engine, even one with a low compression ratio. The four-speed gearboxes are rugged but require skill for smooth shifting. The two-wheel-braked cars must be treated with respect, especially the post-1919 examples which are heavier. Royce moved to four-wheel brakes reluctantly and the early system of 1924, though very strong, was given rather light, front-wheel drums which have little heat dissipating quality. Even though the front brakes receive not more than forty percent of the braking force, the front drums heat rapidly.

The maintenance of a Ghost is very time-consuming; oiling points are everywhere. A complete lubrication of a Ghost will take about a day. Furthermore, the vast amount of copper pipework in the engine compartment presents a constant challenge to the owner-polisher. Ghost ownership is a demanding way of life.

Mechanical adjustment, fortunately, is straightforward and the car presents no impossible novelties. However, Royce favored many little bolts to "knit" parts together; thus, work on these cars may take unusually long periods of time. Furthermore, the occasional complexity of design to produce the "perfect" result often leads to extended repair times. Labor was cheap in 1925!

Problem Areas

The Silver Ghost was designed for long life and absolute reliability. Over the years this car has delivered very high mileages under great abuse. Apart from sheer wear through neglect, very little goes wrong with the Ghost. Failure to lubricate the "great sphere," a massive universal joint in the center of the car, may cause galling and result in driveline rumble. The valve train is entirely reliable but stems may occasionally hang up after long storage. Also the clutch may stick if not blocked open. The reputation of the Rolls-Royce was rightly established by this tough car.

Special Coachwork

Rolls-Royce built no bodies for any pre-1939 cars but was very interested in how the various coachbuilders utilized the chassis. The long engine compartment of the Ghost guaranteed good proportions. And even the big limousines have a stateliness that perfectly represents "British perpendicular." The light-bodied London-Edinburgh-type tourers are perhaps the finest-looking sporting cars of the pre-1914 period.

Buyers should be aware that many early Ghosts have been rebodied—some with work of exquisite quality and others with downright crude work. The presence of authentic body name plates does not guarantee originality. Some of these "replica" bodies are meticulous copies of original coachwork and will, perhaps in time, become indistinguishable from genuine early bodies. In many cases, such bodies represent the saving of an early chassis. Happily, the high value of early Ghost chassis has tended to make cheap reconstructions self-defeating. In any case, a genuine original body is almost always preferable. Rolls-Royce enthusiasts will generally be eager to provide information on cars they are selling, including coachwork reconstruction, in the interest of the truthful preservation of the marque. But it must be emphasized that there are very few pre-1914 Silver Ghosts with complete original bodies, fenders and instruments. Check documentation of "restored" examples with great care.

Summary and Prospects

The Silver Ghost is the supreme example of the Rolls-Royce motorcar and has earned a central place in automotive history. The survival percentage has been fairly good though Ghosts were still being scrapped in the fifties. The relatively large production of 6,173 units of the British model makes availability possible for the serious buyer.

The value of the Ghost has risen steadily and steeply since 1960 in part because restoration costs have skyrocketed in recent years. The pre-1914 cars are now much sought after by collectors and prices have broken the $200,000 level; an honest specimen with original coachwork can hardly be found under $100,000. Late British Ghosts have risen commensurately and prices of fine specimens with attractive bodies are approaching $100,000. Even perpendicular saloons are rarely found below $50,000.

Since the Silver Ghost is the target car for many Rolls-Royce collectors, there is little doubt that demand will be steady and prices will continue to rise, perhaps steeply. This great car provides high owner-driver satisfaction and offers the opportunity for experiencing reliable trouble-free motoring in a 1907 design. The charm of driving a very high geared Edwardian motorcar is hard to exceed.

A magnificent 1914 Barker open-drive limousine, 54AB, with typical Barker fenders. Such original and stately specimens are rare and expensive. Robin Barnard photo.

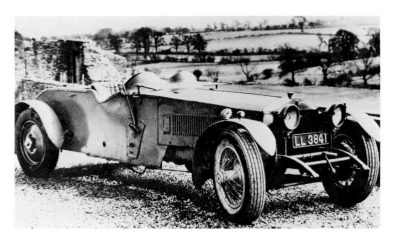

Silver Ghosts occasionally fell into the hands of "boy racers" who refitted the chassis with sometimes bizarre results. This 1910 model, number 1456 (left), could properly carry the factory term "bedeviled," a car whose mechanical integrity and coachwork had been so compromised that Rolls-Royce Ltd. would not touch it. In 1958 a replica tourer (right) was constructed on chassis number 1456. It was a vast improvement on the crude two-seater racing body but lacked the subtleties of a genuine 1910 body. Robin Barnard photos.

This 1912 Ghost, number 1962, was used as a garage breakdown truck from 1930 to 1947. The present body, represented as a London-Edinburgh tourer, was constructed in 1958. The fender valances, high radiator and cut of the top should be kept in mind when comparing it to the genuine article. Value is average. Robin Barnard photo.

This 20RB was modified into a tourer in 1958. Traces of the 1914 body still remain, including the splendid front fenders. The value of the car has certainly been enhanced and, as replicas go, it is not unattractive. Robin Barnard photo.

This Ghost, 20RB, was originally a 1914 Barker cabriolet. In 1925 this rather commercial-looking body was installed by James Bartle of Nottinghill for Lord Ludlow. It was used in this form by Luton Fire Brigade in 1940. The body prevents this Ghost from having a high value. Robin Barnard photo.

The Silver Ghost engine was nearly indestructible due to the massive design, generous bearing dimensions, very low compression and modest rev capabilities. This engine, number S138, was fitted to a 1924 Ghost, 22LM, and was the final form with the late small distributor and water pipework. A major engine rebuild could cost as much as $10,000. Robin Barnard photo.

BRITISH SILVER GHOST

Number produced: 6,173

Original Specification: 6 cylinders (2 blocks of 3), side valves, 4½x4½ (7036 c.c.), cone clutch, 4 speeds, dual ignition with magneto and trembler coil, footbrake external contracting on propeller shaft, handbrake internal expanding on rear drums, suspension semi-elliptic front and platform rear, wheelbase 135½' or 143½', chassis weight 2050 lb. or 2200 lb., tires 875 x 105 (f) and 880 x 120 (f) and 895 x 135 (r), price about £980. bhp: 50-70.

Year	Numbers / Notes
1907	60539-60592 Semi-elliptic rear suspension, 60581
1907/8	60700-60799
1908/9	919-1015 Friction shock absorbers
1909/10	1100-1199 3 speeds, mechanical air pump, 4½ x 4¾ (7428 c.c.)
1910	1200-1299
1910	1300-1399
1910/11	1400-1499
1911	1500-1699 Vibration damper
1911	1700-1799 Torque tube axle
1912	1800-1999
1912/13	2000-2699 Cantilever springs from 2100 on, 4 speeds introduced at 2400
1913	CA 1-20 Double rear wheel brakes, chassis tie rods
1913/14	NA 1-58
1914	MA 1-56
1914	AB 1-67
1914	EB 1-60 3 speeds discontinued, 895 x 135 tires
1914	RB 1-68
1914	PB 1-65 Large carburetter standarized, threaded union
1914	YB 1-66
1914	UB 1-67
1914	LB 1-68
1914	GB 1-49
1914/15	TB 1-37 & 55
1915	BD 1-32
1915	AD 1-32
1915	ED 1-34
1915/16	RD 1-35
1915	CB 1-37
1915	PD 19-33
1915	AC 1-28 Modified chassis
1919/20/21	X 1-16 Show models only
1919	PP 1-36 Air pump on governor casing, 5½' radiator, electric starter and lighting, non-trembler coil, priming device
1919	LW 1-48
1920	TW 1-81
1920	CW 1-102
1920	FW 1-121
1920	BW 1-165
1920	AE 1-141
1920	EE 1-141
1920	RE 1-81
1920	PE 1-81
1920	YE 1-81
1921	UE 1-81
1921	LE 1-81
1920/27	WO 1-279 Armoured car chassis
1920/21	GE 1-81
1921	TE 1-81
1921	CE 1-107 Some numbers used by Springfield
1921	NE 1-123 Some numbers used by Springfield
1921/22	AG 1-182 Some numbers used by Springfield
1921	LG 1-198 Some numbers used by Springfield
1921/22	MG 1-213 Some numbers used by Springfield
1921	JG 1-76 Some numbers used by Springfield
1921/22	UG 1-97 Some numbers used by Springfield
1921	SG 1-91 Some numbers used by Springfield
1922	TG 1-94 Some numbers used by Springfield
1922	KG 1-43 Springfield used 276 KG to 400 KG
1922	PG 1-44
1922	RG 1-43
1922	YG 1-81
1922/23	ZG 1-81
1922/23	HG 1-102
1923	LK 1-100 51-100 duplicated by Springfield with "S" prefix
1923	NK 1-100
1923	PK 1-63 Springfield used 201 PK to 300 PK
1923/24	EM 1-135 Front wheel brakes
1924	LM 1-71
1924	RM 1-103 Late cars were of 144' or 150½' wheel base, had 33 x 5 tires and Autovac
1924	TM 1-103
1924/1925	AU 1-141
	EU 1-129

Of the 20 Silver Ghosts in Melbourne Brindle's lavish book, perhaps nine are extant. This Schapiro-Schebera skiff, 54PB, is one of them. The body was constructed by the Berlin coachbuilder about 1920. Robin Barnard photo.

Hooper built this formal and very perpendicular collapsible town car about 1922. Some collectors fancy its period charm and the rather rakish windscreen, though the erect A-type steering was meant strictly for chauffeurs. Robin Barnard photo.

History

Ghost chassis were assembled at Springfield, Massachusetts, beginning in 1920, in an effort to broaden sales in the United States. The initial production of twenty-five cars was identical to the British Ghost but specifications were gradually Americanized to suit local climate and driving conditions and to take advantage of both U.S. quality and lower prices in component manufacturing.

The introduction of left-hand drive in 1925 (on chassis number S101MK) was an obvious improvement, but the three-speed transmission offered at the time had very wide gap ratios between all gears. And although American Bosch, Bijur and Westinghouse electrics were of superb quality, the move from a 12-volt to a 6-volt system in 1924 (chassis S201KF) could only have been a backward technical step. The Springfield Ghost generally lagged behind the chassis improvements fitted on the British Ghost. For example, American Ghosts were not offered with four-wheel brakes and, indeed, the first few Springfield Phantom I's still had two-wheel brakes. The introduction of the Autovac in England in 1924 was not copied in America until the Phantom I. On the other hand, the American Ghost was fitted with valve covers, a desirable improvement over the exposed-valve British design.

The quality of construction of the American Ghost chassis was superb and, in the opinion of one of the principal British works managers, superior to the Derby product. This was due in part to the opportunity to establish a new plant with more favorable work conditions and to the enthusiasm and initiative of the American mechanics. The Springfield Rolls-Royce is a unique blend of the best of British and American practices.

Identification

The presence of American equipment, especially electrics, is one quick clue; and after 1925, the left-hand drive and three-speed ball change are instant identifiers. The more obvious characteristic, however, is the distinctive and consistent line of the coachwork, principally by Brewster. The great drum headlamps and tubular bumpers are unique to American production. Serial numbers are mixed, with Derby production blended in the early models, and precise identification requires detailed reference material.

Performance and Utility

The American Silver Ghost engine in its final form produced about 85 bhp at about 2300 rpm on the test bed. With the high-speed 3.25 axle, 2300 rpm was just 70 mph. By 1925, however, most Ghosts were offered with the 3.71 ratio to compensate for growing body weight, which meant only 61 mph at 2300 rpm (assuming in all cases 33x5 tires). The Ghost engine is not all that comfortable above 2000 rpm so that really usable speed from these cars is more in the neighborhood of 50 to 55 mph. Fuel consumption will be about 10 to 12 mpg. Acceleration will be leisurely and the gearbox is heavy.

Maintenance is lengthy, tedious and needed regularly. The two-wheel brakes must be kept in good adjustment and used carefully. The car is immensely strong and should give long and reliable service.

Problem Areas

As with the British Ghost, the Springfield car has no glaring weaknesses and, given regular maintenance and lubrication, has nearly unlimited life. The American Ghost has been given much attention in the *Flying Lady*, the publication of the Rolls-Royce Owners' Club, especially in the early years after 1952, and owners will find the back issues of this magazine (still available) a valuable guide in maintenance and troubleshooting.

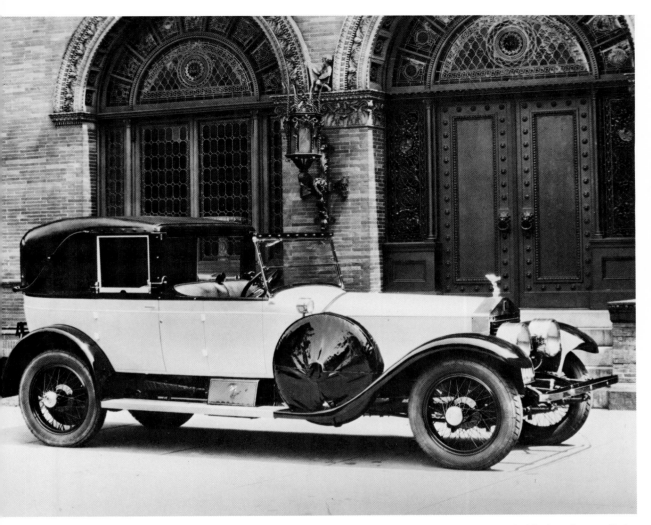

Rolls-Royce Custom Coachwork produced this handsome Sala-
manca for the early Silver Ghost. The car is fully collapsible (convertible) though was most often used in this form for formal work.
The many buttons for snapping on the top are visible beneath the
roof material. The chauffeur's speaking tube is visible in the center
of the front seat. Rolls-Royce Ltd. photo.

Special Coachwork

There is no question that the coachwork on the Springfield Ghost was of exceptional merit and quality. The several basic body types sold as Rolls-Royce "custom coachwork" were laid out by a single team, which gave a consistent identifying look to the Springfield car. To be sure, independent American coach-builders built on the chassis much as their English counterparts did, but the central production became somewhat standardized by 1923 and even more so after 1925 when Brewster and Company was purchased by Rolls-Royce of America. Ernest Hives, later chairman of Rolls-Royce, put it simply, "The best American bodies are better built and better finished than the English. They were made to more practical designs and have better fittings."

A typical Rolls-Royce custom coachwork body on a late Ghost, of whatever type, had a balance and elegance that was hard to beat. The hingework on the doors was heavy and indestructible. The restoration of these cars does not often require the sort of basic wood replacement common to the British coachwork of the thirties, not only because of basic quality but because the sparse and taut lines of the twenties were better suited to resist water thrown up than those of the overhanging sills and exposed surfaces of the later semistreamlined styling.

It is difficult to find an ugly Springfield Ghost.

Summary and Prospects

The Springfield Ghost, along with the Springfield Phantom I, formed the backbone of the original Rolls-Royce Owners' Club in America long before extensive importation began. These cars were often uncovered with very low mileage and many superb examples were given early attention by collectors. The chance of finding good American Ghosts is still reasonable, though prices have come a long way from the few hundred dollars that were required in 1950.

Furthermore, the chance of finding examples with original and unmodified coachwork is good. A few Ghosts have been "lowered" or "sectioned" in a vain attempt to modernize them, the modifications usually done in the early thirties. Some have suffered fender alterations, again in the interest of "modernizing." Some of this damage can be undone easily, but avoid cars that are unrestorable to original specifications.

The chance for future appreciation is mixed, in part because these Ghosts have already reached very substantial prices. Open-coachwork cars, as usual, bring premium prices, but the Brewster closed cars have great charm and, of course, when new, commanded higher prices.

The Springfield Ghost market has moved upward with the British Ghost market. Attractive open-coachwork examples in perfect condition are edging toward six figures. But perfection is not usually the case and the bulk of sales occur around $60,000 to $80,000. Closed cars trail, but fine examples are bringing $50,000. Many European buyers are now importing these cars, a clue to where the market is going.

It may be noted that the Classic Car Club of America looks unfavorably upon cars built before 1925. The American Rolls-Royce with coachwork designed in 1922 and 1923 carrying through 1926 is thus in the peculiar situation of being eligible for classic status after 1924, despite being virtually identical with earlier models. This fact might be useful when buying American Ghosts.

The popular Pall Mall tourer as fitted to the early Silver Ghost by Rolls-Royce Custom Coachwork. The balance of design and perfectly cut top are above criticism. Rolls-Royce Ltd. photo.

The Silver Ghost Piccadilly roadster was another very popular open car in the early and mid-twenties. The beautiful drum head-lamps matched by the side lamps were a splendid addition to a fine design. Rolls-Royce Ltd. photo.

The Tilbury sedan as fitted to the Silver Ghost was a handsome owner-driver body and found many buyers. Such coachwork is often overlooked by collectors seeking more sporting, open bodies. The elegance of this design is hard to beat. Rolls-Royce Ltd. photo.

SPRINGFIELD SILVER GHOST

Number produced: 1,703

The first nine series of Springfield cars used chassis numbers drawn at random from Derby production. The BG series was used exclusively by Springfield, but there was no definite sequence of numbers. These cars (CE through BG) may be identified by their engine numbers: 20-1 through 20-275. bhp: 65.

1921	CE, NE, AG, LG, MG, JG
1921/22	UG
1922	SG, TG, BG
1922/23	276-400 KG
1923	301-425 XH
1923	326-450 HH
1923	51-175 JH
1924	176-300 KF Six volt electrical system from 201 KF
1924	301-400 LF
1924	401-450 MF
1925	S 51-100 LK
1925	S 101-200 MK L.H. drive. 3 speeds: Double battery ignition.
1925	S 201-300 PK
1925	S 301-400 RK
1925	S 401-408 FK
1925/26	S 109-225 ML
1926	S 226-325 PL
1926	S 326-403 RL R-R tubular bumpers. Vertical slat shutters.

Springfield engine numbers—Until 1923, engine numbers were coded to show year of production followed by sequence within the year. Thus, 21-56 is engine 56, made in 1921. Starting in 1923, engine numbers were coded to show year of production and chassis number. Thus, 21548 is an engine made in 1928 (first and last digits) and fitted to chassis S154FR (middle digits).

The following Derby chassis numbers were assigned to Springfield:

CE: 102-107
NE: 112-123
AG: 7, 11, 15, 19, 22, 26, 30, 33, 36, 39, 42, 45, 48, 51, 53, 57, 60, 63, 66, 69
JG: 4, 9, 15, 21, 26, 30, 35, 39, 44, 49, 55, 58, 63, 69, 74, 78, 82, 87, 93, 96, 98, 103, 107, 112, 116, 122, 128, 133, 142, 147, 151, 155
KG: 276-450
LG: 4, 7, 14, 16, 19, 22, 27, 30, 35, 39, 43, 46, 50, 53, 58, 63, 67, 72, 49, 79, 83, 87, 90, 94, 97, 100, 105, 108, 111, 114, 119, 123
MG: 5, 9, 14, 19, 24, 28, 33, 39, 42, 46, 50, 55, 59, 63, 68, 73, 77, 82, 85, 89, 95, 99, 103, 108, 112, 117, 120, 125, 131, 136, 140, 143
SG: 5, 9, 14, 19, 23, 28, 34, 39, 43, 47, 51, 55, 59, 63, 68, 74, 78, 82, 85, 89, 94, 99, 103, 108, 112, 116, 120, 124, 128, 132, 136, 140
TG: 4, 7, 10, 14, 18, 22, 26, 30, 34, 36, 40, 45, 75, 53, 58, 63, 67, 71, 75, 79, 83, 87, 91, 95, 99, 105, 109, 114, 119, 124, 128, 133
UG: 2, 5, 8, 12, 15, 18, 21, 24, 27, 30, 33, 36, 39, 42, 45, 48, 51, 53, 56, 59, 62, 65, 68, 70, 73, 76, 80, 83, 86, 90, 93, 96

History

The Silver Ghost was clearly aging in the early twenties, so the announcement of the New Phantom in May 1925 came none too soon. The new engine had a bore of 4¼ inches and a much longer stroke of 5½ inches with a 7668 cc capacity. Royce modernized the new engine in many ways with overhead valves, the carburetor located on the same side as the induction system, and an automatic ignition advance system. The new engine produced about 100 bhp in its initial form.

The chassis was similar to the Ghost. In the light of the current chassis of the Twenty model, modern by comparison, it was apparent that the Phantom was something of an interim model and, as it turned out, had a relatively short production run.

Identification

The Phantom I was fitted with vertical radiator shutters, unlike the British Ghost which had no factory-fitted shutters whatsoever and the Twenty which at that time had horizontal shutters. Apart from some differences in the engine compartment, early Phantoms were quite similar to the late Ghosts. The cantilever springs were now usually hidden.

Performance and Utility

The New Phantom was a much better performer than the Ghost and could reach 75 mph, and with appropriate light coachwork, perhaps 80 mph. The general running gear was about the same as the Ghost. Steering, however, was heavier, in part because of increased tire sizes and greater weight. The oil gun system of lubrication was continued from the Ghost, which meant many hours of maintenance for chauffeur or owner.

Problem Areas

The New Phantom retained all of the hard-wearing capabilities of the Silver Ghost with one exception. At chassis CL1 (1928), an aluminum cylinder head was fitted to replace the iron head. Though detonation was reduced, the aluminum head has proved to be of limited life. Cracking and leakage resulted in the early scrapping of many Phantoms. Replacement heads are now available. Check oil sumps for water, and water systems for oil.

Special Coachwork

The Phantom I was a transitional model, with coachwork not unlike that of the late Ghosts yet with new styles appearing in 1928 and 1929. The cantilever springing made for a rather high-set chassis so that the coachbuilders were challenged to build a truly low car. Many of the late Phantom I's were quite pretty but it was not a time of genuine innovation.

Be on the lookout for rebodied coachwork on the British Phantom I. Low chassis prices have attracted coachbuilders who strip off big, ugly limousines and usually fit tourers or roadsters. Some are attractive but many examples are garish and inappropriate. Such rebodied Phantom Is cannot have a great future and their sale depends on unwary buyers.

Summary and Prospects

The British Phantom I has been a neglected model in the Rolls-Royce pantheon. It has remained in the shadow of the Silver Ghost which it so much resembles because, despite better performance, the handling of the Phantom I seems heavy and clumsy by comparison. Weight was rising. Front-wheel braking and balloon tires brought their penalties in heavier steering. There was little to commend the New Phantom.

In Britain, especially, the Phantom I was relegated to obsolescence in the early postwar period by Crewe and the service depot at Hythe Road. In contrast, the Phantom II was considered a "modern" car. The problems with the Phantom I's aluminum heads after thirty years did not help the situation.

British Phantom I's could be very conservative and this 1926 Park Ward limousine, 20TC, is typical. It is understandable why such coachwork was not much sought after by collectors for many years. Robin Barnard photo.

The production of replacement aluminum heads has helped the Phantom I market. Prices are now moving upward, not perhaps as strongly as the Ghosts but nevertheless with good prospect. A few superbly bodied sporting Phantom Is can command upwards of $100,000, such as those tiger-hunting cars equipped for Indian princes with handsome original touring bodies, free-standing Grebel searchlights, gun racks and so on. Be on the lookout for counterfeits. The substantial gulf between these high-valued specimens and the top-heavy limousines tempts coachbuilders. Bargain-basement rather upright Phantom I saloons are becoming ever harder to find and are being reevaluated for their period charm.

The Phantom I remains a great motorcar able to evoke much of the motoring moods of a gentler day with speed and elegance.

Hooper is responsible for this handsome 1927 Cabriolet on chassis 94LF. Sporting open coachwork on the British Phantom I is rare and this style would bring top money. Ted Reich archives.

BRITISH PHANTOM I

Number produced: 2,212

Original Specification: 6 cylinders, overhead valves, 4¼ x 5½ (7668 c.c.), single plate clutch, 4 speeds, dual ignition with magneto and coil, 4 wheel brakes with servo plus independent hand brake, suspension semi-elliptic front and cantilever rear, wheelbase 144 or 150½, chassis weight without spare wheel or lamps 3996 lb., tires 33 x 5 (straight side), price £1,850 or £1,900 for long chassis. bhp: 113.

Year	Series	Notes
1925	MC 1-125	
1925	RC 1-125	
1925	HC 1-122	
1925/26	LC 1-132	
1926	SC 1-121	
1926	DC 1-121	
1926	TC 1-121	
1926	YC 1-121	
1926/27	NC 1-121	Front hydraulic shock dampers
1927	EF 1-101	Well base wheels, 7.00 x 21 tires
1927	LF 1-102	
1927	RF 1-101	Rear hydraulic shock dampers
1927	UF 1-101	
1928	EH 1-101	
1928	FH 1-101	
1928	AL 1-101	
1928/29	CL 1-103	Aluminum cylinder head
1928/29	WR 1-132	Side by side rear brakes
1929	KR 1-132	
1929	OR 1-91	

Thrupp & Maberly was responsible for this two-seater on the 1929 chassis 580R. The extremely tight coupe line accentuates the great length of the car, though the balance is probably better with the top down. All coupes are desirable because of their relative rarity; dropheads even more so. Robin Barnard photo.

Barker constructed this Pullman limousine de ville in late 1926 on chassis 102NC. It has a rather more graceful line than was common at the time. Robin Barnard photo.

History

The introduction of the New Phantom in Britain made the American-built Ghost at once obsolete. The necessity of producing a left-hand-drive car at Springfield forced a redesign of the New Phantom engine, specifically to move the carburetor and manifolding to the left-hand side of the block so that the intricate Royce linkages from the base of the steering column could be readily connected. Thus, no Phantom I's were produced at Springfield until late 1926 and even then the first sixty-five examples were still offered with two-wheel brakes, virtually all of which were later modified to the four-wheel system.

The three-speed transmission was retained with central ball change. It was a rugged box, well mated to the new long-stroke flexible engine. In other aspects, the Phantom I chassis was very similar to the Ghost.

In 1928 the aluminum-head engine appeared (S101FR). Production continued strongly until the introduction of the Phantom II in Britain in 1929. Though the Phantom I production was assumed completed by 1931, cars were assembled as late as 1933. The Brewster factory on Long Island, beginning in 1931, fitted bodies to left-hand-drive Phantom II's imported from Derby.

Identification

Early Springfield Phantom I's are externally indistinguishable from late Ghosts. Brewster coachwork was augmented with new models such as the Newmarket convertible sedan in 1927, and a general re-styling of all models was completed by 1929. The conical Hall lamps appeared in 1929 along with flat bumpers. Springfield serial numbers begin with an S.

Performance and Utility

The Springfield Phantom I, with four-wheel brakes and a much more powerful overhead-valve engine, was a great improvement over the Ghost and strong sales reflected buyer approval. By far the most useful new feature of this Phantom I was the Bijur one-shot lubrication system which did away with the laborious lubrication maintenance of the Ghosts. The Springfield system was adopted by the British company for the Phantom II's and is a rare example of American Rolls-Royce technology leading the parent factory. The Phantom I, however, was still only a faster Ghost in chassis layout and the long cantilever springs could be less than stable at the new higher speeds.

Fuel consumption was lower because of the increased efficiency of the new ohv higher-compression engine but owners, eager to use the power, could be forgiven for noticing little difference.

The Phantom I is a very heavy car and is better suited to longer runs and tours than to local use.

Problem Areas

The Springfield Phantom was just about indestructible until the later aluminum heads began to fail. These heads have now been remanufactured and are readily available. Though most lubrication was cared for by the one-shot system, the "great sphere" still required gear oil every 500 miles which was overlooked by many, resulting in wear or rumble, or worse. The Autovac fuel system for bringing fuel forward from the rear tank can give trouble, as well.

Special Coachwork

The splendid beginnings of American coachwork on the Ghost were enhanced on the Phantom I. The gradual addition of body styles such as the gorgeous Ascot and Derby phaetons, not to mention the late Riviera town car (among many others), brought Brewster coachwork to a pinnacle of perfection. The unity of these designs gave to the American Rolls-Royce a readily identifiable "look" which was extraordinarily handsome.

It is thus no accident that the Springfield Phantom was an early favorite among American collectors, because the coachwork was instantly identified as "classic." The British Phantom I's were, on

This Newmarket convertible sedan on chassis number S210KR is a handsome example of Brewster coachwork. The body was later available with a slanted front windshield, although it is hard to improve on the unity of this design. This car rightly commands a high price. Author photo.

Hibbard & Darrin was responsible for this handsome 1929 town car. The top was possibly collapsible since the firm specialized in open coachwork. The massive hingework detracts from the design, but prices should be strong. George Moffitt photo.

balance, not nearly as handsome, in part because the many coachbuilders were freer to indulge the idio-syncrasies of both their own designers and their customers. True "special coachwork" outside of the normal Brewster offerings is rare and may have particular interest to collectors.

Summary and Prospects

In the 1957 register of the Rolls-Royce Owners' Club, there were about 357 Springfield Phantom I's listed in all forms which constituted about one-third of the total number of cars registered. This one model was the original backbone of the American club. In the 1981 register there are only 283 Springfield Phantom I's, which constitute under five percent of the total number of cars in the club.

Though the reasons for the decline in absolute numbers is not altogether clear, it is apparent that the Springfield cars were unearthed early in the game, and one can conclude that the age of their owners may be higher than the general average, assuming owners have retained their cars.

Another implication is that the Springfield cars were restored earlier and maintained better than many other models. None were likely in ordinary use in the fifties, as many British models were in their homeland. Thus, the chance of finding good examples is probably higher than average.

Early recognition, however, does imply early appreciation. As the market inevitably broadened and other models were "discovered," the Springfield Phantom I cars no longer held their pre-eminent position. Comparisons were made by many enthusiasts in the areas of mechanical refinement—and on this score the Springfield Phantoms were judged heavy and "trucky." The sense of lightness found in many Ghosts was gone. But few Rolls-Royce models were as consistently handsome as the Spring-field Phantoms.

Prices for the best examples, such as the Ascot Phaeton, have risen sharply in recent years and can approach six figures. Open-front town cars are also popular. These very good looking Phantoms are finding increasing favor as one of the most handsome automotive expressions of the twenties. There is an opportunity here. Closed-bodied Springfield Phantom Is can still be bought in average con-dition for $30,000 and up, making them attractive entry-level classic cars for enthusiasts. The value of these cars will steadily increase as the collecting market rediscovers the great merit of the Phantom I.

SPRINGFIELD PHANTOM I

Number produced: 1,241. bhp: 113.

1926	S 400-465 FL	Overhead valves, iron cylinder head, centralized chassis lubrication, vacuum fuel feed, four wheel brakes
1927	S 66-200 PM	
1927	S 201-300 RM	
1927	S 301-400 FM	De Jon ignition from S 336 FM
1928	S 101-200 RP	
1928	S 201-300 FP	
1928	S 301-400 KP	20 x 7 tires. External valances
1929	S 101-200 FR	Aluminum cylinder head, chro-mium plating
1929	S 201-300 KR	Conical lamps, flat bar bumpers, automatic shutters, swinging trunk racks
1929	S 301-400 LR	
1930	S 401-500 MR	
1930/31	S 101-241 PR	

The Brewster Kenilworth sedan on this Phantom I chassis was the owner-driver equivalent of the earlier Tilbury design. The Kenilworth was much lower and more angular, in keeping with styling trends. Among closed cars, this design would certainly rate very high, especially when compared to larger limousines. Twenty were built. Rolls-Royce Ltd. photo.

Brewster built many different town cars, a very popular style in the Phantom I production. This St. Regis was a seven-passenger model with a noncollapsible rear section. Twenty were built. Open-front town cars will bring higher prices than fully enclosed limousines. Rolls-Royce Ltd. photo.

Continentals: ★★★★
Others: ★★★

History

The Phantom II was introduced in September 1929 and was a thoroughly up-to-date car. Though engine dimensions were the same as the Phantom I, the new engine was much different in both detail and primary design. A crossflow head helped raise bhp to around 120 at 3000 rpm despite an initial compression ratio of only 4.75:1. Later engines managed 158 bhp with higher compression and a different carburetor. Many details of the engine were revised and improved. Typical of Royce attention to detail was the new vacuum pump which withdrew air from the Autovac independent of any manifold vacuum, thus eliminating fuel starvation on long, steady climbs. Despite this improvement the size of the reserve tank on the Autovac was not reduced.

The chassis was up-to-date. The transmission was finally mated directly to the flywheel housing, the starter now working against the ring gear. The torque tube drive of the Silver Ghost and Phantom I was abandoned, replaced by Hotchkiss drive with a hypoid axle and the cantilever springs were replaced by half-eliptics. The chassis was lower and provided a much better platform for the coachbuilders which made possible the superb body designs marking the pinnacle of the classic era in the early thirties. One-shot lubrication was introduced on the Derby-built car, at first only a partial system but by 1931 covering every nonrotating fitting.

The Phantom II received many changes during its production life of six years, in part because the automobile, industrywide, was in revolution. Synchromesh gearing appeared on third and top gears in 1932 (46MS) and on second gear in 1935 (101TA). High-lift cams (at 102MY, deleted at 101TA), higher compression (2MY) and new controllable dampers (162PY) came along in 1933. Tire size started at 7.00x21, went to twenty inches in 1930 with chassis 169GN, and shrank to 7.00x19 by 1933 (2MY).

Production of the Phantom II ceased in the summer of 1935 though isolated deliveries continued into 1936.

Identification

The Phantom II has a higher radiator than the Phantom I and the chassis is lower, which give an altogether more formidable appearance. The instrument panel was redesigned so that the various gauges were grouped together with a black background under glass. Half-elliptic springs with shackling at the very back of the car are an instant identifier. The massive radiator was still mounted directly above the I-beam front axle which served to retain the classic long hood proportions that make the Phantom II so attractive. Serial numbers are consistent. Left-hand-drive export models on chassis series JS and MS are preceded by the letter A and most carry Brewster bodies. The special Continental series is absolutely identifiable by chassis number.

Performance and Utility

The Phantom II was a modern car in many ways and was so considered by Rolls-Royce in the post-1945 period when full service and spares were maintained. The car was much faster than any previous Rolls-Royce; it was capable of 92 mph in light Continental form, but more usual top speeds were in the low eighties. The Phantom II was very heavy, with weight up to three tons. Fuel consumption was high. The one-shot lubrication system, even in the early partial form, saved vast hours of lubrication time.

There may be no more rugged, reliable car than the Phantom II, which retains all of the best of Rolls-Royce coupled with good though conventional suspension. The car may be driven at high highway speeds with complete satisfaction.

Problem Areas

The Phantom II had one fundamental problem which remains its Achilles' heel, namely the high-lift camshaft. For those cars built between 102MY and 101TA, the chance of trouble is serious. The cam

The rather baroque interior of 9JS, the "Yellow Rolls-Royce" is not typical of the usual Phantom II. The thermos and decanter set are very unusual and the windshield-mounted lamps may be unique. This car must rate high in entertainment, both on and off the screen. Rolls-Royce Ltd. photo.

This yellow Rolls-Royce, a 1931 Barker, number 9JS, was used in the motion picture of the same name. A second Phantom II, not a Barker, was disguised and used as its stand-in and was later sold in England. A lot of yellow Rolls-Royces began to appear soon after! The original 9JS has very substantial value, by virtue of its movie role. MGM Studios photo.

profile is rather sharp and causes galling and scuffing of the followers, which may be detected by a small knocking noise, usually passed off as a tappet adjustment problem. Cam life could be very short, as low as 20,000 miles, though many Phantom II's were able to put up much bigger mileages without trouble. The repair is very expensive, requiring major dismantling of the engine. Numerous suppliers and garages have come up with answers for this specific problem, but the best answer probably is a reversion to the low-lift cam, if one can be found. Buyers of these chassis should pay particular attention to engine noises.

As with so many of the prewar models, the aluminum cylinder heads may be corroded. Watch for leaks and compression loss.

Special Coachwork

The Phantom II offered a splendid chassis for the coachbuilders on both the 144- and 150-inch wheelbases. No longer faced with the high cantilever spring rear suspension, coachbuilders worked hard to produce new body designs, especially in the shrinking market of the Depression years. The Continental chassis was particularly tempting since it attracted owner-drivers who often specified sedanca, drophead or coupe designs. The early Continental sports saloon was equally attractive.

The elegance of the Phantom II can hardly be bettered and the rather sustained production into 1935 of what had become an outmoded chassis design meant a prolongation of the "classic" look. The Phantom II's proportions were maintained by the long hood and radiator set well back over the front axle.

Be on guard for replica or bedeviled bodies on the Phantom II. Gaudy tourers and roadsters or sedans that have been cut into coupes do not have much future value.

Summary and Prospects

The Phantom II was the last model designed by Henry Royce and contains, in its most developed form, all of his ideas going back to the Silver Ghost. The subtle perfection of this car, as seen in the endless details of controls, carburetion and ignition systems, is a delight to all owners. It is an old-fashioned car, the chassis design without innovation and well behind the competition by 1935. Likewise, the engine no longer has the silkiness of the old Ghost because of higher compression and camshaft design. The great weight of the car largely nullifies the increased power and the Phantom II can be a handful in any situation requiring quick maneuvers. But a 144-inch-wheelbase Continental with a compact body is a wonderful high-speed touring car and, in the eyes of proud owners, typifies the finest of early post-vintage motoring.

The Phantom II had a rather slow initial appreciation in the fifties and sixties, in part because it was relatively unwanted on its native soil. Very many were exported to America where the senior Rolls-Royce series was earlier appreciated due to the presence of many Springfield Silver Ghosts and Phantom I's. The Continental model has achieved special interest among collectors because of the superb proportions of almost all the coachwork found on this fine chassis. Prices for these Continentals have moved to the very top of the Rolls-Royce market for nearly all models.

Be sure to check that any Continental is genuine, by the use of the chassis number list in the Appendix of the RROC directory or with Gentile's *The Rolls Royce Phantom II Continental*. Most mundane Phantom IIs can be bought on the low side of $50,000 and many will be in the $20,000 to $30,000 region, especially since there are still numerous unrestored or even rough examples on the market.

The Phantom II can expect gradual appreciation. Fuel prices have made this car fiercely expensive to use, especially in Britain, which may offer opportunities to buyers from time to time. Apart from the camshaft problem and occasional aluminum-head trouble, the Phantom II is virtually indestructible.

The Brewster bodies mounted on nearly all of the AJS and AMS left-hand-drive series were very attractive, particularly such rare styles as the Henley roadster. But the creative effort was largely spent by 1932 though production continued in 1933 and ended in early 1934. Meanwhile, the great British coachbuilders were moving ahead with inspired designs such as the Owen sedanca. The short-chassis Continental attracted especially handsome bodies. As a result, the left-hand-drive cars, despite their utility, have not shown a particular price premium.

Jensen Hojrup of Denmark constructed this body perhaps in 1957 on a 1930 chassis, number 71XJ. The beautiful lamps are from a much earlier period. Rebodied cars of a later style have limited value, whether mounted on the Phantom II or other chassis. Robin Barnard photo.

In 1931 H. J. Mulliner constructed this metal Weymann saloon on chassis number 49GX. It is a good example of the typical close-coupled saloon on the Continental chassis. The flared front fenders are especially attractive. Robin Barnard photo.

Hooper offered this car on the Phantom II chassis in the fall of 1933 at the Olympia show on chassis number 20PY. The Philco radio is mounted in the center of the panel and cost 45 pounds. The fabric paneling on the jump seats follows a design used by Hooper throughout the thirties in its formal coachwork. Hooper & Co. Ltd. photo.

This short-chassis drophead coupe by Fountains of Horsham, number 82XJ, brought 36,000 pounds at Christie's Auction House in 1981—a very high price for the time. The car had done only 9,000 miles. Patrick Bogue photo.

H. J. Mulliner built this sedanca coupe in 1934 on chassis number 120SK. At some time the original fenders were removed and the pontoon replacements were fitted as shown. They rather dominate the car and give it an entirely new character. Collectors usually opt for originality. For a picture of this car as first constructed see *Those Elegant Rolls-Royce* (page 149) by Lawrence Dalton. Bob Barrymore photo.

Park Ward produced this very smooth sports saloon for the Continental chassis. Robin Barnard photo.

The interior of the Brewster Newport town car on the Phantom II was of the highest quality. Brewster often favored loose seat squabs. The triangular motif in the woodwork was another typical styling feature. Rolls-Royce Ltd. photo.

PHANTOM II

Number produced: 1,767

Original Specification: 6 cylinders, overhead valves, 4¼ x 5½ (7668 c.c.), single plate clutch, 4 speeds, dual ignition with magneto and coil, 4 wheel brakes with servo plus independent hand brake, suspension semi-elliptic front and rear, wheelbase 144 or 150, chassis weight without spare wheel or lamps 3810 lb., tires 7.00 x 21, price £1,850 or £1,900 for long chassis. bhp: 120.

1929/30	WJ 1-133	
1929/30	XJ 1-204	
1930	GN 1-202	20 x 7 tires from 169 GN
1930	GY 1-207	
1930-31	GX 1-68	
1931/32	JS 1-86	Thermostatic shutters
1931/32/33	AJS 201-303 (L. Hand) Despatched as follows: 201 AJS - 276 AJS 1931, 277 AJS - 288 AJS 1932, 289 AJS - 303 AJS 1933	
1932	MS 2-170	
1932/33/34	AMS 201-224 (L. Hand) Despatched as follows: 201 AMS 1932, 202 AMS - 206 AMS 1933, 207 AMS - 209 AMS 1932, 210 AMS - 220 AMS 1933, 221 AMS - 222 AMS 1934, 223 AMS - 224 AMS 1932	
1933	MY 2-190	19 x 7 tires
1933	MW 3-115	
1933/34	PY 2-206	Controllable dampers from 160 PY
1934	RY 3-211	
1934	SK 2-196	
1934/35	TA 1-203	
1935	UK 2-82	

The following were despatched as P-11 Continental Chassis. Four were long wheelbase: 89RY, 128SK, 190SK and 97TA

EX: 26 (prototype)
GY: 82, 104
GX: 6, 28, 31, 40, 41, 42, 43, 44, 45, 46, 47, 48, 49, 50, 51, 52, 53, 54, 55, 56, 57, 58, 59, 60, 61, 62, 63, 64, 65, 67, 68
AJS: 256, 287
JS: 1, 4, 8, 11, 12, 20, 24, 33, 34, 35, 39, 60, 63, 64, 65, 72, 73, 74, 80, 81, 82, 83, 84, 85
AMS: 207, 208, 209
MS: 2, 4, 20, 24, 28, 32, 36, 48, 50, 54, 58, 60, 64, 66, 70, 72, 74, 76, 80, 86, 88, 90, 98, 100, 104, 106, 114, 116, 118, 122, 124, 132, 148, 150, 158
MW: 3, 7, 15, 19, 25, 31, 33, 39, 41, 45, 47, 55, 57, 69, 71, 73, 99, 101, 103
MY: 2, 8, 10, 14, 16, 20, 24, 26, 32, 56, 58, 62, 64, 72, 74, 80, 82, 90, 92, 94, 106, 116, 118, 124, 126, 128, 130, 134, 140, 142, 156, 166, 170, 172, 176, 182, 186
PY: 2, 4, 8, 22, 24, 30, 32, 36, 42, 44, 52, 54, 62, 64, 66, 70, 72, 74, 82, 84, 86, 90, 92, 94, 98, 104, 106, 118, 136, 142, 144, 154, 156, 158, 160, 162, 164, 180, 204, 7, 9, 15
RY: 23, 37, 47, 49, 55, 57, 59, 71, 77, 79, 83, 85, 89, 97, 99, 101, 109, 117, 119, 121, 125, 127, 139, 143, 147, 149, 153, 155, 157, 159, 165, 169, 175, 185, 189, 191, 197, 201, 203
SK: 2, 4, 6, 8, 14, 18, 24, 60, 68, 70, 86, 88, 90, 92, 94, 96, 99, 101, 103, 109, 119, 120, 128, 138, 154, 170, 188, 190
TA: 17, 21, 25, 27, 29, 45, 53, 97, 103, 109, 123, 131, 149, 161, 179, 187
UK: 5, 42, 50, 62

This very pretty coupe, 144PY by Thrupp and Maberly, should command a top price. Robin Barnard photo.

History

The introduction of numerous V-12 and V-16 engines in American luxury cars, not to mention the great Hispano Suiza J12 series, made the Phantom II six-cylinder engine increasingly anachronistic. Furthermore, the development of independent front suspension which, by 1936, was fitted to even cheap American cars, set new high standards for riding comfort which the Phantom II could not equal.

In response to these challenges, the new Phantom III was announced in the fall of 1935, and it was a very substantial break from Rolls-Royce tradition. The engine was a marvelous V-12 unit of 7340 cc displacement, offering 165 to 180 bhp at 3000 rpm. Wet liners and marine-type connecting rods not unlike those in the KB Lincoln were paired on six throws of the crankshaft which was set in seven main bearings. Twin coil ignition, hydraulic valve lifters and the triple pressure oiling system were typical of Rolls-Royce refinement.

The chassis was entirely new and featured the General Motors-type independent front suspension, but with an enclosed oil chamber around the coil spring. The result was a superb riding and handling car, altogether smoother than the Phantom II and with performance enhanced—even with very heavy coachwork. The Phantom III was a marvel of technical ingenuity and the designers did not shrink from complexity in their search for perfection.

Identification

The Phantom III is instantly identifiable by the massive, forward-mounted radiator, no longer directly above the old beam axle as on the Phantom II. The classic proportions of the Phantom II were lost as Rolls-Royce embraced a modern idiom of design. The eighteen-inch wheels with big 700 or 750 tires are noticeable. The instrument panel of the Phantom III is covered with many switches and the effect can be intimidating. And one look at the V-12 engine under the hood confirms the unique specifications of this model.

Performance and Utility

The great Phantom III had immense high-speed capabilities and could maintain 80 mph in continuous reliability. Top speed was initially just below the Phantom II Continental, about 90 mph, but acceleration was better. Later overdrive models could just touch 100 mph. But the fascination of the Phantom III was in the total smoothness in which this great car could come up to such speeds, quite unlike the six-cylinder Phantom. The car was and remains very modern in performance.

Fuel consumption was high, as might be expected from performance with great weight. Controls were smooth and remarkably light so that driving was a pleasure. Maintenance was somewhat complicated and, in the case of engine lubrication and filtration, rather critical. Braking was excellent.

The massive appearance of most of the Phantom III's, despite an eight-inch-shorter wheelbase than on the Phantom II, was derived from the frequent fitting of formal coachwork which this chassis attracted. Such formal cars were not readily usable outside of their intended function. Owner-driver Phantom III's with compact coachwork and the even rarer semisporting body types enhanced the pleasure of this superb model.

Problem Areas

The Phantom III engine has been a source of major trouble for collectors. Unless the engine is chemically protected, the mixture of alloy and iron tends to promote corrosion. The engine "eats itself up." Failure to keep the oil very clean causes early breakdown of the hydraulic valve clearance system. Sediment in the block, in part from corrosion, causes spot overheating and is responsible for the V-12's poor cooling reputation.

Freestone & Webb produced this very streamlined saloon on 3AZ68 in 1936. It must have given
a good account of itself in high-speed touring.
Such advanced coachwork was not that common
on the Phantom III. Robin Barnard photo.

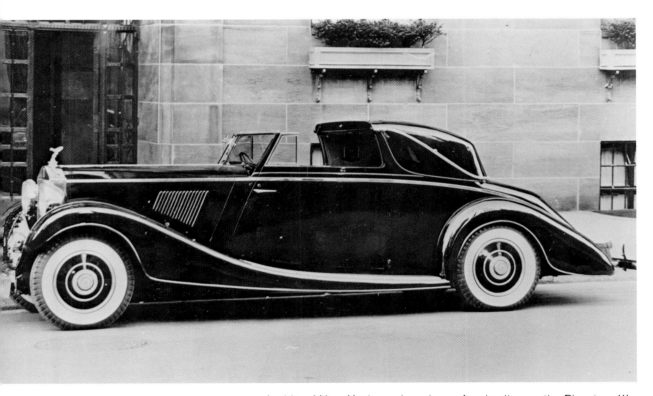

Inskip of New York produced very few bodies on the Phantom III,
and this is a superb example of its sedanca coupe. It ranks well
against the best European coachwork and should command a top
price in the Phantom III market. George Moffitt photo.

The sheer complexity of the engine hastened the junking of these cars much before the small-horsepower models; and by the time collecting values reached the point that made a worn Phantom III salvageable, many examples had been lost. Engine rebuilding cost remains awesome and beyond the capabilities of most restorers and garages.

This savage set of circumstances has depressed the Phantom III market for a very long time despite the superb specifications of the car. Desperate owners have fitted the eight-cylinder postwar B80 engine and even more desperate owners have resorted to any power plant that offers reliability. It is critically important that buyers of the Phantom III make a detailed investigation of engine history and rebuilding quality because the Phantom III's charm is centered in its great and troublesome V-12 engine. Bastard engines of any heritage reduce the value of the car greatly.

Special Coachwork

There may be no more sumptuous coachwork than that fitted to the Phantom III. The chassis offered an immensely strong platform and the forward mounting of the engine made possible new opportunities for creative coachbuilders. Also, the immediate prewar years were the final fling of the private coachbuilders operating on an older set of economic rules. Original buyers of a Phantom III were hardly interested in skimping, and lavish specification was the rule.

Phantom III coachwork is often "heavy"; that is, simply, big. There are indeed brilliant graceful saloons, sedancas and the rare coupes. More likely one encounters the D-backed limousine which may have done honorable hire work or given quiet solace to many bereaved families as a funeral car. In any event, there were no prewar Rolls-Royces capable of transporting more people in greater comfort.

Summary and Prospects

The Phantom III remains an enigma among Rolls-Royce collectors. It is at the summit of Rolls-Royce prewar engineering and remains a car of regal specification. Yet even when the car was in production it made little money for Rolls-Royce and the complexity of design and construction doomed the model in a high-labor-cost postwar environment. The Phantom III may be regarded as the Rolls-Royce *tour de force*, a splendid folly never to be repeated.

Collectors have long since retreated with respect from the prospects of maintaining the V-12 engine and only the most knowledgeable and dedicated owners make up the hard core of Phantom III enthusiasts. This is the reason for the continued modest prices of the Phantom III when compared to other cars with similar specifications. It remains a bargain when measured by first price. But any mechanical maintenance is extremely expensive and the decayed engine which one can still encounter may be virtually unrestorable.

The Phantom III is rare, not only because of its low production but also because of its modest survival capacity. It may well turn out to be the rarest Rolls-Royce of them all, with the exception of the Phantom IV and the pre-Silver Ghost early cars.

Owners desiring to be a part of this exclusive group must be prepared to embrace the idiosyncrasies of the Phantom III with enthusiasm and a full purse.

Future depreciation is uncertain because the appearance of cars needing work offered at "knocked down" prices seems to bring down the price of really good specimens. In the longest perspective, however, the Phantom III must surely find its true high price based on its intrinsic worth and rarity.

Hooper constructed this saloon on 3AX199. The trunk was a bit overpowering and must have been awkward to load—there was no opening lid! The idea was to protect the interior of the car from dust, as the car was intended for use in Kenya. Frank Dale photo.

Park Ward was on target with this beautiful sedanca de ville on 3BU48 built in 1937. A more graceful formal car could hardly be imagined. The very neat razor-edged trunk and rear body sweep are exceptional. Frank Dale photo.

Windovers was probably the constructor of this sedanca de ville on chassis 3AZ62. The rear pillarless construction is especially attractive. Frank Dale photo.

This Hooper body on 3BT133 lacks a certain unity, particularly around the rear door. It is no match in style to 3AZ62. Frank Dale photo.

All Weather Bodies built this four-door convertible on 3AZ76. Coachwork of this class has a special attraction despite the bulky rear appearance of the converted top. Prices are high. Robin Barnard photo.

PHANTOM III

Number produced: 710

Original Specification: 12 cylinders (V-12), overhead valves, 82.5 mm. x 114.3 mm. (7338 c.c.), single plate clutch, 4 speeds, dual coil ignition, 4 wheel brakes with servo plus independent hand brake, suspension independent front with enclosed coil spring and semi-elliptic rear, wheelbase 142, chassis weight without spare wheel or lamps 4050 lb., tires 7.00 x 18, price (chassis) £1,850. bhp: 165-180.

1936	3 AZ 20-238	
1936	3 AX 1-203	
1936/37	3 BU 2-200	
1937	3 BT 1-203	
1937	3 CP 2-200	
1937/38	3 CM 1-203	Petrol pump in frame from 3 CM 35
1938/39	3 DL 2-200	18 x 5 tires from 3 DL 78 Overdrive from 3 DL 172
1939	3 DH 1-11	

This striking convertible coupe by H. J. Mulliner on 3AZ132 is unique. The very small passenger area accentuates the great bulk of the car. Two-seater coachwork is very unusual on the Phantom III and commands high prices. Robin Barnard photo.

History

At the end of 1920, the post-World War I collapse of the luxury car market reached the point at which the future of the Silver Ghost was in question. The development of a smaller Rolls-Royce to broaden market appeal was hastened and the first new "baby" Rolls-Royce appeared in 1922. With engine dimensions of 3x4½ inches, the six-cylinder overhead valve unit displaced 3127 cc and developed 53 bhp at 2750 rpm. A three-speed central ball change transmission plus a central handbrake brought some criticism, a specification changed in 1925 (GPK I) to right-hand four-speed gate change with right-hand brake lever in the fashion of the British Silver Ghost. Two-wheel brakes give way to excellent four-wheel brakes with servo-assistance at the same time. The small car was well received and the company, perhaps unwittingly, set the stage for its long-range future; the engine's cylinder center distance remained the same until the end of six-cylinder production in 1959.

Identification

The Twenty was much smaller than the Ghost. In the beginning it had horizontal radiator shutters, which were changed to vertical in 1928 (GFN 1). The two-wheel brakes and center change until 1926 are instant identifiers. The later Twentys were often similar to the early 20/25's and must be identified by the chassis number plate.

Performance and Utility

The Twenty's charm lies in its "sweetness." The early models are very light on the controls and are charming to drive. But they are dead slow. Even with the lightest of tourer bodies the cruising speed is not much higher than 45 mph although the top speed may approach 60. Burdened with heavier coachwork, the Twenty labors under any hilly challenge. When driven within its limits, the car will last indefinitely. At such low speeds the two-wheel brakes are not really a problem, but the four-wheel system after 1926 is much better despite a slight increase in steering effort. The four-speed box was a very important change and helped to compensate for the low engine power. The Twenty is a car that may be driven regularly in modest local use. A driver needs an unhurried attitude to long distances.

Problem Areas

The very low stresses in the Twenty, the result of low power and low rev limits, make this car very durable. The engines can deliver very high mileages unless overrevved in the gears (top gear overrevving is hardly possible). But occasional freeway efforts by overenthusiastic new owners have been known to destroy engines, in particular those with filled crankshaft sludge traps. Head cracking is not uncommon because the casting is long and light and sediment build-up produces spot overheating. New reproductions are available (at the time of this writing) at around $4,000. The running gear seems to be indestructible.

Special Coachwork

All Twentys carry coachbuilt bodies though some, like the lovely Barker barrel-side tourer, were built in batches. A light body is essential to savor the pleasures of the Twenty, and the Weymann construction used at the end of the decade in some closed cars is desirable. Tourers and coupes are especially "right" for the Twenty. There are few really ugly bodies on the Twenty; the period perpendicular styles are well suited to the speed limits of the model. Even the heavier limousine and landaulet bodies somehow manage to convey charm.

Summary and Prospects

The Twenty was a latecomer into the U.S. market; perhaps fewer than fifty were in the country as late as 1958. The modest size put off collectors who knew only the big Ghosts and Phantoms. Its meager

Barker built this straightforward sedanca de ville on chassis GSK 46 in late 1925. The open front always adds value and the very private rear section suggests this was a rather special order. Weight was the enemy of the Twenty and the new four-speed gearbox and four-wheel brakes were helpful to this car. Robin Barnard photo.

Hooper built this pretty fixed-head coupe on the 1929 chassis GEN 30. The large back roof panel suggests four seats. Small coachwork, especially with two doors, is desirable on the Twenty and will bring high prices. Ted Reich archives.

performance made the car unsuited to American highways. Prices remained low, not only because of limited demand but because of abundant supply in Great Britain. The Twenty seemed like but a poor man's version of the "real" Rolls-Royce.

The virtues of the Twenty have slowly become appreciated in America and for the knowledgeable collector, who understands the nature and limits of the car, much happiness is in store, as the British have long known. As operating and fuel costs rise, the Twenty will find new admirers who relish the fineness of construction that gives nothing away to the Ghosts and Phantoms. Prices remain well beneath those of the big cars and relative bargains are still to be found. Speculators have usually avoided the Twenty, which has further helped to maintain reasonable prices.

Appreciation in both the short and long runs should be modest but steady. Buy the Twenty for enjoyment of refined vintage motoring.

TWENTY HORSEPOWER

Number produced: 2.940

Original Specification: 6 cylinders, overhead valves, 3 x 4½ (3.150 c.c.), single plate clutch, 3 speeds, coil ignition, independent foot and hand brakes acting on rear wheels, suspension semi-elliptic front and rear, wheelbase 129, chassis weight 2,200 lbs., tires 32 x 4½, price (chassis), £1,100, bhp: 53.

1922/23	40-G-1 - 50-G-0	
1923	50-S-1 - 60-S-0	
1923	60-H-1 - 70-H-0	
1923	70-A-1 - 80-A-0	
1923	80-K-1 - 90-K-0	
1923	GA 1-81	
1923/24	GF 1-81	
1924	GH 1-81	
1924	GAK 1-81	
1924	GMK 1-81	
1924	GRK 1-84	
1925	GDK 1-81	
1925	GLK 1-81	
1925	GNK 1-94	
1925	GPK 1-81	Front wheels brakes, 4 speeds
1925/26	GSK, 1-81	
1926	GCK 1-81	
1926	GOK 1-81	
1926	GZK 1-41	
1926	GUK 1-81	
1926	GYK 1-92	
1926/27	GMJ 1-81	Front hydraulic shock dampers & well base wheels, 5¼ x 21 tires
1927	GHJ 1-81	
1927	GAJ 1-41	
1927	GRJ 1-81	
1927	GUJ 1-81	
1927/29	GXL 1-82	
1928	GYL 1-82	Rear hydraulic shock dampers
1928	GWL 1-41	
1928	GBM 1-82	
1928	GKM 1-82	
1928	GTM 1-41	
1928/29	GFN 1-82	Vertical radiator shutters, 6.00 x 21 tires
1929	GLN 1-87	
1929	GEN 1-82	
1929	GVO 1-81	
1929	GXO 1-10	

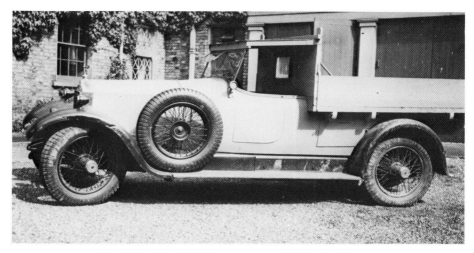

By 1950, this 1923 Barker tourer, 54-S-4, had been reduced to hack service for the Newland Garage in Hull. Win Estes photo.

In 1969, 54-S-4 was rebuilt by Wilkinson of Derby and the rear section was restored. This car today is in California and probably is the best Barker barrel-side tourer in America. William C. Brooks photo.

Knibbs of Manchester offered this close-coupled saloon about
1925. The fabric covering suggests a Weymann-type construction.
Robin Barnard photo.

William Watson constructed this roadster in 1923 (right) on chassis 50-S-6. This car has been given substantial modifications along with a meticulous restoration, and now has a much sportier appearance. Collectors generally prefer originality when considering long-range investment potential. The Watson roadster, 50-S-6, as currently shown (left). Dr. McClain Johnston and Robin Barnard photos.

This H. J. Mulliner fabric saloon, GFN 8, had fallen on hard times when this picture was taken. Small wheels have changed the proportion of the car, the high-mounted lamps are awkward and the fabric is in bad shape. Value of this car is obviously very low. For an original picture see Fasal, *The Rolls-Royce Twenty,* page 398. Robin Barnard photo.

An entirely original H. J. Mulliner Weymann saloon built in 1929 on
chassis GFN 71. This very light body is what the Twenty should
properly carry. The Weymann angularity, lovely wheel discs and
busy windscreen add charm. Robin Barnard photo.

Park Ward's light treatment of this saloon, GFN 82, is about the best approach to putting a lot of coachwork on a small chassis. GFN 82, however, remains all too typical of the saloon styles of the period. Prices are moderate for such coachwork. Robin Barnard photo.

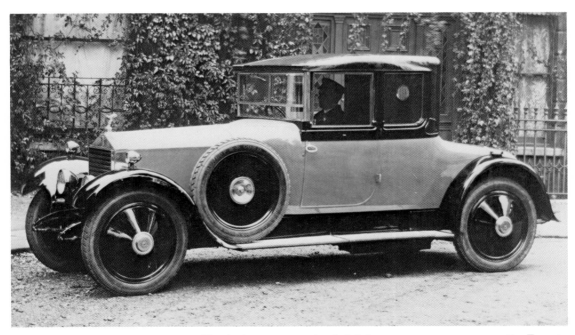

Doctor's coupes and cabriolets were more common on the Twenty chassis, and this neat cabriolet is typical. The light weight of such bodies is well suited to the Twenty, and prices should be strong. John Fasal photo.

History

The Twenty became embarrassingly slow as the decade drew to a close. Not only were motoring speeds generally rising but body weights were climbing. The simplest and most logical response was to rework the fine little engine for more power. Accordingly, the Twenty engine was bored out to 3¼ inches (3699 cc) and given a heavier crankshaft which raised the critical speed to 4000 rpm (in 1922, only 3300 rpm). The compression ratio began at 4.6, increased to 5.25 in 1930 and 5.75 in 1932. Brake horsepower started at sixty-one at 3000 rpm and increased to perhaps seventy at the end of production in 1936. Little else was changed from the Twenty chassis.

Thermostatic shutters appeared in 1932 (GBT22), removing the chore of manual control and careful watching of the water temperature gauge. Synchromesh was on third and top gears in 1932 beginning with GKT22. An electric fuel gauge replaced the temperamental hydrostatic gauge beginning in 1932 with GAU I. The 20/25 was very well received and outsold the Phantom II by more than two to one.

Identification

The small size of the early 20/25's became less obvious as streamlining developed in the mid-thirties and bodies lengthened. Chassis number identification is essential. Though P100 headlamps were sometimes fitted, smaller-diameter lamps are more usual. The standby magneto continued, as well as the small speedometer.

Performance and Utility

The 20/25 was substantially faster than the Twenty and in 1936 could just exceed 75 mph with light coachwork. With the usual rear axle ratio of 4.55:1, the revs at top speed were fearsome and the roar of the cooling fan was pronounced. Cruising speed was more on the order of 55 mph. There were alternate axle ratios available including a 4.16:1 which helped. The car remained on the slow side with a 0-60 time of thirty-one seconds in 1935. The one-shot lubrication system appeared in final form in 1932 on GBT22, greatly easing maintenance chores. The 20/25 is a much more modern car than the Twenty and though it retains a good deal of the charm of the earlier model, it has just enough performance to cope with freeway speeds.

Problem Areas

The 20/25 continued the fine reputation of the Twenty for reliability. Head cracks may still be found now and then and occasionally rear axle troubles are possible. However, many of these cars have slogged along under appalling conditions year after year with virtually no maintenance whatsoever.

Special Coachwork

The development of the streamlined body occurred during the run of the 20/25 with some rather unfortunate results. The gradual abandonment of the D-back for saloons and limousines led to faired-in trunks, "beaver tails" and many experimental shapes resulting in some downright ugly cars. Coupe and drophead bodies generally were able to make the transition more gracefully. There are some very pretty bodies of all types on the 20/25 but one is more likely to encounter bizarre and idiosyncratic coachwork on this model than on any other Rolls-Royce type.

Summary and Prospects

The 20/25 has survived in large numbers because it was considered daily transportation in Britain until very recently. Many were driven to extinction or were rescued at the brink of total breakdown. Restoration costs have dealt the 20/25 a cruel blow because the investment necessary to restore this car has often exceeded the value of the finished product. The result is that many of these cars remain in

Early 20/25's were very similar to the Twentys. This 1930 Hooper enclosed limousine is typical. The line is untainted by stream-lining and retains the earlier unity. Prices for cars of this style are modest. Robin Barnard photo.

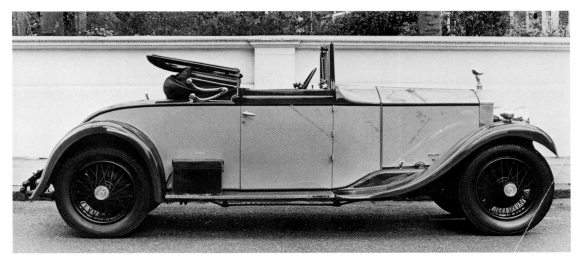

This charming drophead coupe, GXO 92, was built by Thrupp & Maberly in early 1930. It is a fine example of a personal "doctor's coupe" and is much sought after. The first series of the "25" is hardly distinguishable from the last series of the Twenty. Frank Dale photo.

poor condition, investors having favored the Phantoms of the same period. Furthermore, though the 20/25 can show beautiful and even racy lines from time to time, its performance could never match its good looks. It is sad to report that some of these cars are still being broken up for parts.

The discerning buyer with an eye for beauty can still find among the 20/25's some very lovely cars at relatively modest prices. Even the most desirable coachwork—the sedanca coupes by Gurney Nutting, for example, or some of the pretty work by H. J. Mulliner and Freestone and Webb—can be bought at reasonable prices. Few Rolls-Royces will give such honest service and long life as the 20/25, their very virtues having, in some measure, been responsible for so much neglect. Appreciation will be modest because the abused examples or those with ugly coachwork tend to drag the market down for the entire series.

20/25 H.P.

Number produced: 3,827

Original Specification: 6 cylinders. overhead valves. 82.6 mm. x 114.3 mm. (3680 c.c.). single plate clutch. 4 speeds. coil ignition with standby magneto. 4 wheel brakes with servo plus independent hand brake. suspension semi-elliptic front and rear. wheelbase 129. chassis weight 2650 lb.. tires 6.00 x 19. price (chassis) £1.185. Centralized chassis lubrication. bhp: 65.

Year	Chassis	Notes
1929/30	GXO 11-111	
1930	GGP 1-81	
1930	GDP 1-81	
1930	GWP 1-41	
1930	GLR 1-82	3' longer chassis
1930	GSR 1-81	
1930	GTR 1-41	
1930/31	GNS 1-81	
1931	GOS 1-81	
1931	GPS 1-41	
1931	GFT 1-81	
1931/32	GBT 1-82	Thermostatic shutters from GBT 22
1932	GKT 1-41	Synchromesh gearbox from GKT 22
1932	GAU 1-81	Electric petrol gauge
1932	GMU 1-81	
1932	GZU 1-41	
1932	GHW 1-81	
1932/33	GRW 1-81	
1933	GAW 1-41	
1933	GEX 1-81	
1933	GWX 1-81	
1933	GDX 1-41	
1933	GSY 1-101	
1933	GLZ 1-81	
1933	GTZ 1-81	
1933	GYZ 1-41	
1933	GBA 1-81	
1933	GGA 1-81	
1933	GHA 1-41	
1933/34	GXB 1-81	
1934	GUB 1-81	
1934	GLB 1-41	
1934	GNC 1-81	
1934	GRC 1-81	
1934	GKC 1-41	
1934	GED 1-81	
1934	GMD 1-81	
1934	GYD 1-69	Controllable dampers from GYD 25
1934	GAE 1-81	
1934	GWE 1-83	
1934	GFE 1-41	
1934	GAF 1-81	
1934/35	GSF 1-81	
1935	GRF 1-41	
1935	GLG 1-81	
1935	GPG 1-81	
1935	GHG 1-41	
1935	GYH 1-81	
1935	GOH 1-81	
1935	GEH 1-41	
1935	GBJ 1-81	
1935	GLJ 1-81	
1935	GCJ 1-41	
1935/36	GXK 1-81	
1936	GBK 1-81	
1936/37	GTK 1-63	

The instrument panel of a 20/25 as presented on chassis GAU 40, a Hooper enclosed limousine photographed in July 1932. Spark advance, carburetion mixture, throttle and horn were all mounted at the top of the steering column. The switchbox directly above the steering column on the panel controlled side lamps, headlamps and charging rate and contained a push-and-turn instrument panel light switch. Hooper and Co. Ltd. photo.

This dramatic drophead coupe was mounted on chassis GRC 26 in 1934 by Fernandez & Darrin. The coachwork was quite angular, which gave a lightness to the car's appearance. Bob Barrymore photo.

Sometimes even the great coachbuilders came up with "clangers."
This 1935 Barker saloon, GCJ 17, illustrates the problems that
Barker had when it attempted to mate the new streamlined rear
with a very upright door and window area. Sophisticated collectors
find little of interest in this car. Robin Barnard photo.

It is hard to believe that this beautiful coupe by Park Ward on GGA
15 is two years older than the Barker saloon above. It demonstrates
the truth that in buying a Rolls-Royce, coachwork is crucial in
establishing value. Ted Reich archives.

The rakish lines of this 1935 James Young sedanca coupe, GPG 38, were intensified by paint
designs. In 1935 this car was at the forefront of
styling, and remains a very desirable collecting
piece today. Bob Barrymore photo.

This Windovers saloon was mounted on GBJ 72 in 1935. Though
the styling might not appeal to everyone, the car is distinctly sporting and well above the more common perpendicular saloons and
limousines in value. Robin Barnard photo.

This upright Barker saloon is typical of the mid-thirties styling aimed at the conservative British buyer. The Barker quality was evident and many did buy. This car, chassis GCJ 22, has the rear deck folded down and fitted with a handsome trunk—ready for touring. Douglas Brown photo.

Hooper built a well-balanced, close-coupled saloon on the 20/25, of which this is a fine late example. Few closed bodies have aged as gracefully, though top market values remain below those of almost all open-coachwork examples. Robin Barnard photo.

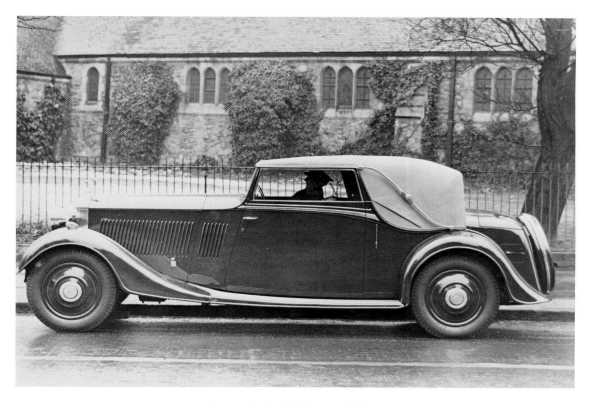

A very desirable Thrupp & Maberly drophead coupe that ranks at the top of the market for 20/25's. By 1935, production of these beautiful personal cars was very limited. Robin Barnard photo.

History

Increased performance was again needed in the small Rolls-Royce by the mid-thirties so the 20/25 was bored to 3½ inches giving a displacement of 4257 cc. The standby magneto was abandoned in place of a standby coil with spare distributor points clipped in a small receptacle attached to the firewall. Carburetion was simplified and twin SU pumps replaced the Autovac. The hypoid axle was continued, having been introduced at the close of the 20/25 production (GTK42). Marles cam and roller steering was less "sticky" and lighter than the worm and nut used on the 20/25. A Stromberg carburetor was fitted. In other respects the 25/30 retained most of the previous specifications.

Identification

Very early 25/30's were identical in appearance to the last 20/25's. By 1937 the large, round speedometer appeared which was common to later models. Also in early production the Autovac was replaced by twin SU fuel pumps mounted on the firewall in the engine compartment. The horn area of the steering column was much simplified and no longer carried the carburetor controls. The horn button was larger and was marked "loud/soft."

Performance and Utility

The 25/30 is substantially faster than the 20/25 and can be cruised comfortably at 60 mph or more, with top speed about 80 mph. Weight was rising, both for chassis and coachwork, and speeds were slower for heavy bodies. The SU pumps, despite their occasional well-publicized failures, gave good service and forever banished the fuel starvation possible on long, full-throttle hill climbs with the Autovac. This model remains even more usable in present-day service than the 20/25. Maintenance routines are very minimal, with the fine one-shot lubrication system.

Problem Areas

Head problems are possible and reproductions are available but at a price. Axle half-shafts are subject to fatigue breaks because of the higher power, and their small diameter, though problems rarely appeared in the first decade or two of service. The SU pumps can be individually tested by a dash switch that should give warning when trouble is pending.

Special Coachwork

The coachwork of the late thirties was much more integrated not only because the stylists had recovered their way, but because some of the provincial coachbuilders that had supplied the odd bodies had gone out of business. The 25/30 carried a higher proportion of formal coachwork than the 20/25, in part because the Phantom III was such a formidable purchase as an alternative and the 25/30 proved to have enough power to carry the heavier limousines. The new, longer wheelbase of 132 inches provided further reason. Close-coupled saloons were generally attractive as the solutions to trunk styling were reached. Open coachwork was now much rarer. The "sedanca coupe" is ultra rare and valuable.

Summary and Prospects

The 25/30 was the last traditionally sprung Rolls-Royce; trouble free, a bit stiff and without vice. This car has continued to give excellent service and driving pleasure. Short production life makes it generally a bit rarer than the 20/25 and it has managed to retain the sense of "modernity" better than the previous model. The great difficulties with the Phantom III maintenance helped sell the 25/30, as wealthy owners found in the smaller car little sacrifice in payload and luxury with a happy bonus in long, trouble-free running. This perhaps explains why much formal coachwork has survived in respectable condition on this chassis. The 25/30 has never suffered from being so cheap as to encourage neglect.

H. J. Mulliner built this neat razor-edged saloon in 1937 on GRP 36. Its style was carried through into the postwar period. Small owner-driver saloons such as this are not only pretty but very driveable. Robin Barnard photo.

This late-1936 Thrupp & Maberly coupe, GRM 42, was originally a drophead. The large and low rear window was a bit odd but was the only way to harmonize it with the existing belt line. Coupes generally bring higher prices than saloons, especially on the small 20/25 chassis where light weight is important. Frank Dale photo.

Investors and collectors have found in the 25/30 a pleasant and very driveable prewar Rolls-Royce, which is sometimes mistaken for the Phantom III by casual observers. The Phantom III was shorter than the Phantom II and lacked the very long, commanding hoodline, while the 25/30 was longer than the 20/25. The difference between the senior and junior models was indeed less than before.

Appreciation potential of the 25/30 is good, especially if one can find the small owner-driver saloon or personal coupe or drophead. The ubiquitous limousine is easier to find and consequently of less value.

This flashy sports saloon on GXM 29 was Freestone and Webb's fine effort in 1937. Coachwork on the 25/30 is generally pretty staid and this car should command a strong price. Ted Reich archives.

25/30 H.P.

Number produced: 1.201

Original Specification: 6 cylinders. overhead valves. 89 mm. x 114 mm. (4257 c.c.). single plate clutch. 4 speeds. coil ignition with standby coil. 4 wheel brakes with servo plus independent hand brake. suspension semi-elliptic front and rear. wheelbase 132. chassis weight 2900 lb.. 6.00 x 19 tires. price (chassis) £1.100. Stromberg carburetter. S.U. petrol pumps. bhp: 85.

1936/37	GUL 1-82
1936/37	GTL 1-81
1936/37	GHL 1-41
1936/37	GRM 1-81
1936/37	GXM 1-81
1936/37	GGM 1-41
1936/37	GAN 1-81 New type steering controls
1936/37	GWN 1-81
1937	GUN 1-41
1937	GRO 1-81
1937	GHO 1-81
1937	GMO 1-41
1937	GRP 1-81
1937	GMP 1-81
1937	GLP 1-41
1937/38	GAR 1-81
1938	GGR 1-81
1938	GZR 1-41

This solid Barker touring saloon, GRM 15, dates from 1936. The vent panes in the front and rear windows add interest and, with the smooth belt line, lift the car above the more typical Barker offerings. Robin Barnard photo.

Barker was nearing the end as an independent coachbuilder when it built this formal saloon on GRP 1 in 1937. It was typical of Barkers in the mid-thirties which were often fitted with divisions. The conservative line has not aged as well as that of the close-coupled saloons, though interiors may be sumptuous. Prices should be modest. Frank Dale photo.

History

The introduction of independent front suspension on the Phantom III made a similar system inevitable on the smaller cars, and in 1938 the new Wraith was so fitted. The chassis was completely redesigned and fitted with hydraulic jacks pumped from within the car. The engine was given the crossflow cylinder head similar to the 4¼ Bentley and the timing gear train was simplified. Ignition advance was entirely automatic. The gear lever was less obtrusive and the handbrake was repositioned beside the driver's seat, activated with a "pull up" motion. The emphasis on the Wraith was refinement and it may well be the quietest Rolls-Royce ever built. The radiator was moved forward, as part of the suspension changes, allowing a bit more space for the coachbuilders; but the classic "radiator over front axle" relationship was lost. The Wraith design was thus entirely up-to-date and looked ahead; it was not just another revision of the original Twenty.

Identification

The forward-mounted radiator and independent front suspension instantly define the Wraith externally. The stubby, bent brake handle and short gear shift lever are quite unlike the previous small cars. The Wraith is sometimes confused with the Phantom III, though when put side by side the difference in size is apparent. An immediate clue is the wheel nuts. The Wraith, like the Derby Bentleys, had simple eight-sided nuts while the Phantom III retained the more complex traditional Rolls-Royce center-locking nuts. Another difference is that the Wraith hood or bonnet sides have two ventilator doors while the Phantom III has three. Wraith tires are 6.50x17 while the Phantom III has big 7.00x18's.

Performance and Utility

Despite engine refinements, the Wraith is little faster than the 25/30, partly because of increased frontal area. The ride is superior though steering is a bit slower with less of the vintage feel. Most owners thought this a great improvement. The controls and general behavior of the car can only be described as "silky" and the car is virtually silent. The Wraith is a masterpiece of balanced design and the car returns great pleasure to owners.

Problem Areas

The new independent front suspension can occasionally give trouble if maintenance is neglected. The old I-beam axle suffers any abuse but the Wraith needs regular use of the one-shot lubricator and topping-up of the hydraulic shock-absorber body. The engine has shown very good, long-running life. The running gear seems to be very reliable, though gearbox problems may arise from bearing wear which will show up in occasional slipping out of gear.

Special Coachwork

A short production run and the gathering clouds of war cast a somber note over the Wraith, and the coachbuilders, ever shrinking in number, hardly had a chance to bring fresh imagination to designs for this fine chassis. It would sometimes seem that virtually all Wraiths had either a limousine or a four-light saloon body. The forward placement of the radiator posed few problems for formal coachwork but the very few coupes and dropheads were sometimes awkward and bulky. Wraith bodies tend to be heavier, in fact, in general appearance.

Summary and Prospects

Because of its short production life, the Wraith remains one of the rarest of all Rolls-Royces. Its technical specification is different from all other models. Built to prewar standards, it remains the final refinement of the small car theme. Wraiths are gentle cars, marvelously quiet with good ride qualities. Too many Wraiths are burdened with heavy formal coachwork, but the smaller saloons and coupes are

This H. J. Mulliner limousine on WLB 14 was a fine effort to get as much body as possible on the Wraith chassis. Though better than most limousines of the period, such coachwork probably has less value than the best of the owner-driver saloons. Robin Barnard photo.

James Young built this handsome razor-edged saloon in 1939 on WHC 80. Few Wraith saloons are prettier. Frank Dale photo.

altogether delightful to drive. Wraiths are becoming harder to find as more collectors discover their virtues. Prices are slowly climbing, though limousines may still be bargains. Be careful of heavily used examples—many Wraiths have never been out of service since 1939. Mechanical restoration costs may be higher than normal because many Wraith parts are unique.

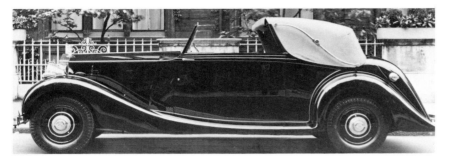

Drophead coupes are rare on the Wraith and this example by James Young is exceptionally handsome. It is very similar to WMB 70 on the opposite page but the contrasting top color and slightly sharper line at the rear bow reduces the bulky effect. The price will be very high. Ted Reich archives.

This splendid James Young saloon coupe on WMB 38 shows off the razor-edge styling and narrow pillars to good effect. The same style body was also fitted to the Bentley and the Phantom III. A Wraith could hardly look better. Ted Reich archives.

WRAITH

Number produced: 491

Original Specification: 6 cylinders, overhead valves, 89 mm. x 114 mm. (4257 c.c.), single plate clutch, 4 speeds, coil ignition with standby coil, 4 wheel brakes with servo, suspension independent front with enclosed coil spring and semi-elliptic rear, wheelbase 136, chassis weight 3040 lb., 6.50 x 17 tires, price (chassis) £1,100, bhp: 90.

1938/39	WXA 1-109
1938/39	WRB 1-81
1939	WMB 1-81
1939	WLB 1-41
1939	WHC 1-81
1939	WEC 1-81
1939	WKC 1-25

The new proportions of the Wraith are well shown by this James Young coupe, WMB 70, which was originally a coupe de ville. The forward mounting of the radiator enabled the body to be enlarged, but in the process the car became "heavy." It is a graceful car but lacks the proportions of earlier models. Such coachwork is very rare on the Wraith and brings a high price. Robin Barnard photo.

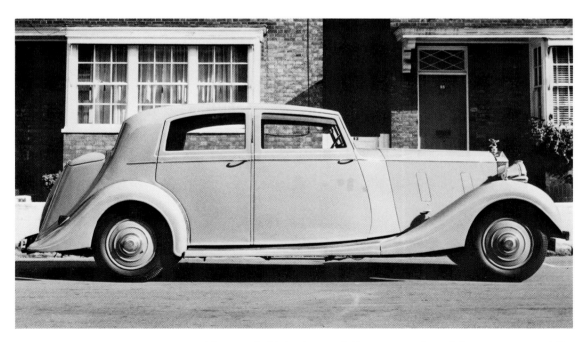

Thrupp & Maberly used the crowned roof line on many of its saloons mounted on Bentleys and Phantoms as well as on this pretty Wraith WHC 27 built in 1939. The car is well proportioned and the body complements the new chassis. Frank Dale photo.

1921-1929 3-liter ★★★★
1926-1930 6½-liter ★★★★★
1927-1931 4½-liter ★★★★★
1930-1931 4½-liter (supercharged) ★★★★★
1930-1931 8-liter ★★★★★
1931 4-liter ★★★

History

The term "Vintage Bentley" describes the cars made by W. O. Bentley as an independent manufacturer prior to the purchase of the firm by Rolls-Royce in 1931. These cars have no technical relationship to Rolls-Royce products and, in the 6½- and eight-liter forms, became direct competitors of the Phantom I and especially the Phantom II. The rich racing history and the remarkable durability of the vintage Bentley have attracted many enthusiasts. The Bentley Drivers Club is a venerable organization and gives strong support to collectors, though it places a remarkable emphasis on competition. A cult car such as the vintage Bentley requires careful study by any buyer, and only the most cursory observations may be made here. The bibliography on the Bentley is exceptionally rich and thorough study is essential.

The marque began as a three-liter sports car and over half of the 3,048 total production was of this model. Maximum horsepower for the three-liter was about 85 at 3500 rpm. The 4½-liter variant was up to 110 bhp in touring form. Both of these models may represent the ultimate in high-speed four-cylinder vintage touring. The six-cylinder 6½- and eight-liter models were designed more for refined coachwork, albeit with little sacrifice in performance. Final horsepower of the eight-liter was 200 to 230 depending on compression and tune. The four-liter six-cylinder car built in the final days of the company was something of an anomaly because the push rod engine was quite unlike other Bentley products, all of which had featured an overhead cam. Also, approximately fifty blown 4½-liter cars were produced—which at peak tune produced 240 bhp, but reliability suffered.

All of these models had particular virtues and rather few vices. The vintage Bentley was always tough and lasting.

Identification

All Bentleys have a distinctive radiator shell with a winged B at the top. The enamel color of the badge identifies the model, as follows:

Blue - Small badge. Most 3-liters
     Standard 6½ liter
     1931 8-liter
     1931 4-liter
Red - 3-liter speed model
Green - Short-wheelbase 100 mph 3-liter
     Works team cars
     Racing 4½
     Speed six
Black - 4½-liter, some 8-liters
     Supercharged 4½-liter

There have been many modifications—engine swaps, body swaps and other confusion—especially in the four-cylinder Bentleys. Careful check of serial numbers should always be made with reference to S. Sedgwick's *All The Pre-War Bentleys—As New*, in which every car is shown as originally delivered. Departure from originality can thus instantly be determined.

Performance and Utility

Bentleys are fun to drive and, with the exception of the four-liter, are all bright and fast. Some early, long-chassis three-liter tourers can be a bit pedestrian but are still able to show cruising speeds in the sixties. The blown 4½, in contrast, has blinding acceleration comparable with the finest modern cars. W. O. Bentley personally preferred the big six-cylinder cars which were much smoother and offered every refinement. Bentley enthusiasts are unlikely, however, to overlook the great thumping four-cylinder 4½'s which have a marvelous vitality.

A very pretty three-liter Bentley Speed model displayed at the Kensington Bentley Drivers Club meet in 1974. The rudimentary rear door on the driver's side was rarely used. Ted Reich photo.

VINTAGE BENTLEY		
	No. Produced	bhp
1922-31 3-liter	1.634	70
1922-30 6½-liter	545	140
1928-31 4½-liter (includes six in 1936)	669	100
1930 4½-liter supercharged	50	175
1931 8-liter	100	200
1931 4-liter	50	–

There were seven different gearboxes used in the nine-year production life of the vintage Bentley and there is much interchangeability. The close-ratio boxes, A and D, are more desirable and generally easier to use. The wide-ratio B box is the least desirable for the sporting motorist. The C box has a close third with wider ratios below and the BS variant has a super-close third gear. The F-type box was used in the eight-liter and four-liter cars with ratios slightly closer than the C. Knowledgeable buyers will verify the box type to ensure that downgrading swaps have not taken place. The vintage Bentley, when properly set up, is a reliable motorcar and is often used in rallies, long-distance runs and club circuit racing. Owners, however, do not hesitate to maintain their cars with much care and substantial resources. Given a good car with moderate use, reliability should be very high. The lubrication and maintenance routines are little different from other vintage cars of the twenties.

Problem Areas

Bentleys are often driven very hard and failures of all components can occur. The cross-shaft gears which drive the magnetos are heavily loaded and can break. Engine work often requires the lifting of the block, since the heads are nondetachable, a challenge to all but the adventuresome. Rear axle failures have been known to occur.

After sixty years on the road, one must expect problems now and then, especially with vigorous driving. Parts are in reasonable supply through many specialist firms, but prices are very high.

Again, with gentle use, anathema to so many Bentley enthusiasts, the cars give little trouble.

Special Coachwork

There are few makes which have suffered so many body swaps as the vintage Bentley. A great number of perfectly good saloons have been discarded over the years in favor of the ubiquitous tourer, so often mislabeled as a Le Mans Replica. The typical Bentley buyer wants the wind in the face. In the process, however, many very primitive bodies found their way onto this noble chassis and the results are frequently awful. In the past years some excellent replica coachwork has been produced, especially as the value of the cars has climbed, and cannot be faulted on quality when compared to genuine original bodies.

One approaches all Bentleys with care when checking coachwork. Using the Sedgwick book, first find out what was originally mounted on the car. If the original body remains, then check for modifications, refendering, lamp exchanges to nonvintage types, modern instruments and so forth.

There are some buyers who do not care if a car is not original, especially if they intend to use it in competition. But for highest value, originality remains the most important factor. The further a vintage Bentley has departed from original, the more it must be questioned.

There are very few honest original Bentley saloons remaining among the four-cylinder cars, and these are now being seen for what they really are: perhaps the most charming expression of the vintage period. The same might be said of the coupes and dropheads. The Bentley remains that odd car for which one finds that the most common offering is the tourer.

It is important that any buyer do careful homework on coachbuilding. Johnnie Green's *Bentley, Fifty Years of the Marque* and John Adams and Ray Roberts' *A Pride of Bentleys* make useful pictorial references.

Summary and Prospects

The Bentley market is highly specialized and one is well advised to approach it with thorough study. Membership in the Bentley Drivers Club and the Rolls-Royce Owners' Club (American) is essential in order to build up price information. As is the case with cult cars, sales are frequently private and by word of mouth, which is why club membership is important.

The prices of Bentleys have appreciated steadily for many years, and explosively so in the past five years. There are now very few decent vintage Bentleys under $50,000. Open coachwork in fine condition commands $75,000 or more for four-cylinder cars. Six-cylinder Bentleys with superb coachwork are now in six figures. Famous name cars may bring $300,000 or more. Bentley enthusiasts worry that such price escalation may end the vigorous driving which has always characterized the marque. The cars have become too valuable to use.

Strong parts sources, good club support and cars of great character ensure continuing popularity. Be prepared for high repair costs if trouble comes. Be prepared for marvelous driving pleasure when all is well.

A 1923 Bentley three-liter saloon by Gurney Nutting on the long 10-foot 10-inch wheelbase. This is an exquisite example of British "perpendicular." The chassis number is 203. Ted Reich photo.

A 1929 4½-liter H. J. Mulliner Weymann saloon on chassis NX 3459. Many of these saloons were rebodied with tourers and consequently have become somewhat rare in original form. Ted Reich photo.

Barker is responsible for this handsome saloon mounted on the 1928 6½-liter Bentley. The whimsical mascot is well proportioned to the size of the car. Ted Reich photo.

This superb tourer on the 6½-liter chassis, number FA2518, is a replica and proves that the finest quality work is still available. The leather hood straps and "quick-release" radiator cap are in the spirit of the coachwork. The chassis originally carried a Thrupp & Maberly cabriolet de ville. Ted Reich photo.

The gifted Basil Mountfort restored this lovely 4½-liter tourer, chassis number XL 3105. The chassis originally carried a Freestone & Webb saloon. Few could quarrel with the superb result. Ted Reich photo.

One of the noble 100 eight-liter Bentleys, a 1931 Mayfair coupe on chassis number YX5124. The superb proportions of this car make it seem smaller than the 144-inch wheelbase might suggest. C. G. Heywood took delivery in June 1932. Ted Reich photo.

CHAPTER 13
3½-LITER BENTLEY
1933-1936

History
Replacement for the vintage Bentley was delayed for two years after 1931 as Rolls-Royce struggled to come up with an appropriate car. The solution was found in using a chassis designed for a 2¾-liter smaller Rolls-Royce combined with a modified 20/25 engine. Engine changes included a new crossflow head, twin SU carburetors, higher compression and camshaft reprofiling. The result was a very bright, good-handling, high-speed motorcar. Rolls-Royce refinement caused the new Bentley to be called "the silent sports car." The car turned out to be not only fast, but very long wearing.

Identification
The 3½ Bentley is much smaller than the 20/25 Rolls-Royce and is much lower. After the earliest production, the big P100 headlamps were usually fitted and dominated the frontal appearance of the car. The chassis number plate may be found on the left side of the aluminum firewall by the engine.

Performance and Utility
The 3½ Bentley is a fine performer, especially with early lightweight coachwork. With about 105 bhp, top speed is around 92 mph. One-shot lubrication makes maintenance easy. Driving pleasure is very high, in part because the car is relatively light (Park Ward saloon, 3,350 pounds). The Bentley comes close to being an ideal owner-driver car of the thirties.

Problem Areas
The rear axle, designed for a 2¾-liter car, was overstressed and, after thirty years of hard use, can cause trouble. Half-shaft or driving-dog failure is not uncommon and pinion bearings may suffer. Cylinder heads may deteriorate over the years and cracks are possible. Few other mechanical problems are found in a generally very strong car. Check for rust and decay, especially around rear wheel arches. On very abused examples, frame fracture may have occurred. Bentleys often suffer from hard use and, in general, wear may be accelerated by neglect and abuse. Careful inspection of the body structure, at pillars and rear wheel arches in particular, is essential because the combination of a flexible frame and stiff springing caused terrible racking.

Special Coachwork
Few cars have more graceful coachwork than the Bentleys of the thirties. Truly ugly bodies are noticeable by their rarity. Open coachwork is especially desirable. Happily there are few rebodied cars, and these will have lower value in almost all cases.

Summary and Prospects
The 3½-liter Bentley has been overlooked by collectors for many years, in part because the cars lack the bulk of the big-horsepower Rolls-Royce models and because so many Bentleys remained in service well into the "collecting years." The hard-wearing qualities of the Bentleys made them serviceable without heavy maintenance and many examples became very shabby. There was also a certain snobbery among some Rolls-Royce collectors in which the 3½ Bentley was seen as a second-class Rolls-Royce.

It is becoming more apparent that the 3½ Bentley has an immense charm and that the quality is on a par with anything that Rolls-Royce has produced. It is thus still possible to buy these handsome small cars at favorable prices. Restoration costs will be high but as discriminating collectors discover what may be one of the finest-driving cars of the thirties, future price appreciation of the marque seems likely.

Drophead coupes and tourers have recently shown very greatly elevated prices, often two or three times those of saloons. This may help to draw up the prices of closed coachwork.

This early 3½, B38CR, has a very pretty Barker saloon body. It was originally owned by the Marquis of Bath. The squared-end door handles are typical Barker. Collectors are discovering some of the bargains still available for these lovely cars. Strother MacMinn photo.

Vanden Plas was a master at building a flush-fitting top-down line, and this handsome example on B118LS shows its skills to advantage. Open coachwork like this is much sought after, and brings twice the price of saloons in comparable condition. Frank Dale photo.

This 1934 Hooper saloon is typical of the firm apart from the continued horizontal belt line which, unfortunately, has nothing to do with the rear body and trunk lines. Cars of this general style are common offerings and are fairly priced. Frank Dale photo.

Freestone & Webb was responsible for this very neat saloon, on B190DG. The low sweep of the running boards and the fine frontal appearance gave the 3½ a wonderful aggressive appearance. Frank Dale photo.

The Fisherman's Saloon by Hooper is unusual: It has a removable rear seat and many special fittings. D-backed saloons are extremely rare on the Bentley, and this example may be unique. Frank Dale photo.

The instrument panel of the Bentley was neatly laid out, high-lighted by the large and legible speedometer and tachometer. Rolls-Royce was especially competent on wiring and switch gear. Charles Spangenberg photo.

This 1935 Thrupp & Maberly saloon has the semi-airline tail that was popular in the mid-thirties. Frank Dale photo.

BENTLEY 3½ LITER

Number produced: 1.177

Original Specification: similar to 20/25 (q.v.) except S.U. carburetters and fuel pumps. wheelbase 126. chassis weight 2550
lb.. tires 5.50 x 18. bhp: 105.

1933/34	B 1-203 AE	
1934	B 2-198 AH	
1934	B 1-201 BL	
1934/35	B 2-100 BN	
1934	B 2-200 CR	
1934/35	B 1-203 CW	Controllable dampers
1935	B 2-200 DG	Dunlop wheels
1935	B 1-199 DK	
1935	B 2-200 EF	Rudge-Whitworth wheels
1935	B 1-203 EJ	
1935	B 2-200 FB	
1935/36	B 1-159 FC	

Park Ward was responsible for most of the Bentley dropheads
of which this one, B88FB, on a 1935 chassis, is a fine example.
The balance of the design is evident. Prices for dropheads in restored condition are very high. Charles Spangenberg photo.

 With exceptions

History

The introduction of the 25/30 Rolls-Royce brought a parallel enlargement of the Bentley engine to 4¼ liters (4257 cc). General development occurred continuously on the Bentley and later cars benefited from it. There were no major mechanical changes. The overdrive M series began in October 1938, though there was much overlapping with earlier series in terms of sales dates.

The Mark V first appeared in August 1939 and was a substantially redesigned car with independent front suspension, divided prop shaft and numerous engine changes. The overdrive transmission of the M series was continued, with slight ratio changes.

Identification

There are few external differences between the 3½ and 4¼. The M series has fixed radiator shutters, seventeen-inch wheels and Marles steering. The Mark V is instantly spotted by the forward mounting of the radiator shell and the independent suspension. Chassis number plates are mounted on the left side of the firewall by the engine.

Performance and Utility

All the virtues of the 3½ were enhanced in the 4¼ as bhp rose to 126. Top speed was 96 mph and in the M series, 107 mph. Mark V top speed fell back to 97 mph, a result perhaps of weight and frontal area increases. Fuel consumption was down fractionally. These strong and spirited cars were the final refinement of thirties post-vintage motoring.

Problem Areas

The rear axles were even more overstressed than in the 3½-liter models and trouble is possible. A clunk indicating looseness in the rear axle may be nothing more than a worn driving dog, however. Check operation of thermostatic radiator shutters. A rust and corrosion check both of body and chassis is mandatory.

Special Coachwork

The 4¼ and M series continued to be fitted with exquisite coachwork. Perhaps over 400 of the 4¼'s were fitted with the Park Ward steel saloon, the closest thing to series production achieved by Rolls-Royce before the war. This attractive body added needed strength to a rather flexible chassis but it must be checked for rust, especially around the trunk area. The dropheads again are favorites. Be careful of all open coachwork as it lacks rigidity, and check for evidence of sloppiness in doors which may indicate critical wood rot in door posts. Aluminum may not rust, but does present problems of fatigue, cracking and corrosion.

Summary and Prospects

Like the 3½, the 4¼ has been overlooked and offers great future appreciation if a solid example can be found. The M series cars (only 200 made) are exceptionally desirable. Their ability to cruise at high speeds without fuss makes them candidates for the finest sporting product of Rolls-Royce before the war. The Mark V is so rare as to preclude market estimates, but on the basis of rarity alone it probably should be rated with four stars. Poor examples of all of the above may be found and high restoration costs must be considered. The prewar Rolls-Royce-built Bentleys remain very attractive motorcars for discerning buyers. But already, highly restored examples with special coachwork are very expensive.

This very pretty sedanca was built by Gurney Nutting in 1937 on chassis B129JY. Stylish open coachwork of such marked individuality brings top prices. Frank Dale photo.

B142JD was originally fitted with a Vanden Plas All Weather body in March 1937. This shooting brake body which replaced it lacks both subtlety and style. The value of this car is limited. Frank Dale photo.

The four-door All Weather body was not common; and only about 30 were built on the 4¼ chassis. Vanden Plas' version was very neat, as shown here on B114KT which was delivered in the summer of 1937. Attention should be paid to the fit of doors and windows. Fine examples bring very high prices. Frank Dale photo.

Park Ward built over 400 steel saloon bodies, including this one fitted to the overdrive chassis, B82MR. The chrome wheel discs are a bit brash and would normally be painted. The rear springs on this car are too flat and need re-arching. The steel body adds much needed rigidity to the flexible chassis. Examine the trunk area for rust. A good example of this steel saloon can make a very fine Bentley 4¼ and prices are reasonable. Strother MacMinn photo.

Though the front of this Bentley seems like so many others, keen-eyed observers will recognize one of the rare Mark V's, in this case, B14AW, the only convertible mounted on the series. The radiator is forward of the usual position. Coachwork on this car was by Saoutchik. Frank Dale photo.

BENTLEY 4¼ LITER

Number produced: 1.234

Original Specification: similar to 25/30 (q.v.) except S.U. carburetters. wheelbase 126. chassis weight 2560. tires 5.50 x 18. bhp: 126.

Year	Chassis	Notes
1936	B 2-260 GA	Air cooled dynamo. Filters on rear X member
1936	B 1-203 GP	
1936	B 2-200 HK	
1936	B 1-203 HM	
1936/37	B 2-200 JD	
1937	B 1-203 JY	
1937	B 2-200 KT	
1937	B 1-203 KU	
1937/39	B 2-200 LS	
1938	B 1-203 LE	
1938/39	B 2-200 MR	Overdrive 6.50 x 17 tires
1938/39	B 1-203 MX	

BENTLEY MARK V

Number produced: 14 chassis (13 completed cars)

Original Specification: similar to 4¼ except independent front suspension with open coil springs. wheelbase 124. chassis weight 2720. tires 6.50 x 16. bhp: 126.

Year	Chassis
1939	B10-34 AW

H. J. Mulliner produced this "high vision" saloon in the summer of 1939 on chassis B21MX. A roof window fitted just behind the windshield could be covered by an interior shade. There are several hints of Mulliner's postwar styling in this handsome car. Frank Dale photo.

This rare Mark V, chassis number B30AW, carries an H. J. Mulliner saloon. The forward mounting of the radiator is clear. The wheel disc on the spare wheel suggests that discs would normally have been fitted to the road wheels. David Scott photo.

Park Ward built many drophead coupes on the Bentley 3½ and 4¼; the graceful lines of this fine example on B30HK may explain why. The rear wheel spats are a nice touch. Frank Dale photo.

In the fall of 1938, H. J. Mulliner mounted this fine drophead body on B157LE and featured the folding metal top cover. It was probably the neatest solution to the canvas stowage problem. Frank Dale photo.

In July 1939, H. J. Mulliner built this coupe on chassis B53MX. The exceptional balance and very smooth rear section give this rare car a high value. Frank Dale photo.

The Freestone & Webb "top hat" style, a very sharp razor-edged line, is usually associated with saloons. Perhaps only three such coupes were built and rarity adds to the value of this car. Frank Dale photo.

This group of cars constitutes the major used-car market at the present time. The defining characteristic is the separate chassis, which ended with the introduction of the monocoque Shadow series in 1965. A further breakdown may be made by the two engines used, the six-cylinder unit from 1946 to 1959 and the V-8 from 1960 to 1965.

The early postwar cars were much more homogeneous than the prewar offerings. In 1939, Rolls-Royce produced two distinct models and a Bentley, all quite different. It was apparent to product planners that the postwar market and new, higher production costs could hardly allow such diversity. Accordingly, only two models were offered in 1946, with different chassis but with only one basic engine. The Rolls-Royce Silver Wraith was a chassis available for custom coachwork while the Bentley, though available as a chassis too, was most often fitted with a new pressed-steel body mounted at Crewe, the home of postwar motorcar construction.

The initial diversity of coachwork on both the Rolls-Royce and Bentley chassis was not unlike that of the immediate prewar period. There was every effort to make it business as usual, but there were now only about ten well-known British coachbuilding firms at work and the list quickly shrank as the small provincial houses withdrew. The major firms also weakened: Freestone and Webb closed in 1958; Hooper in 1959; H. J. Mulliner sold out to Rolls-Royce in 1959, then merged with Park Ward in 1961. At the end of 1965, only James Young remained as an independent and its doors closed in 1967.

Thus, the chance of finding interesting and individualistic coachwork is best at the beginning of the postwar period. By the early sixties, virtually everything offered by Rolls-Royce and Bentley was in standardized form. Even the James Young bodies were usually different only in subtleties and interior detail.

The mechanical stability of the postwar car was impressive. The six-cylinder engine was steadily improved, even as it was enlarged, and by 1959, in its final form, there may not have been a better engine ever produced by Rolls-Royce. The beautiful gearbox had lost none of its prewar refinement. The introduction of the Hydra-matic transmission as an option in 1953 broadened the market appeal but soon displaced another of the distinctive and treasured features of the marque. The combination rear mechanical and front hydraulic braking system was satisfactory, but four-wheel hydraulic brakes appeared on the Silver Cloud and Bentley S series, still mated to the well-proven servo system, and with a mechanical back-up system to the rear.

The introduction of V-8 engines in the second series brought new performance levels. The six-cylinder engine, burdened by power steering and, especially, air conditioning, became a marginal performer compared to American V-8 engines. After a suitable teething period in second-series production, the V-8 settled down and in the years from 1963 to 1965 a higher level of reliability was reached. This final production of the traditional chassis-body construction has earned a fine reputation.

The success of the Bentley standard steel saloon and the decline of the independent coachbuilders made a standard-bodied Rolls-Royce inevitable. The Silver Dawn, a Bentley with minor changes, first appeared in 1949 and was the beginning of a total blending of the two marques. By 1955 when the Silver Cloud began, the similarity had reached the point where the two makes were advertised together and the radiator cost became the price differential. Those diffident about being seen in a Rolls-Royce could own a Bentley. But diffidence goes just so far, after which economic motives take over: Once it was realized that a used Bentley sold for far less than a used Rolls-Royce of the same vintage, the fate of the Bentley was sealed.

The percentage of Bentleys produced compared to Rolls-Royces fell dramatically between 1946 and 1965.

Percentage of Bentley to total Crewe production:

Bentley MK VI and R (Compared to Dawn and Silver Wraith to D series)—76%

Bentley S1 (Compared to Cloud I and Silver Wraith E to H series)—57%

Bentley S2 (Compared to Cloud II)—41%

Bentley S3 (Compared to Cloud III)—32%

Bentley T Series (Compared to Shadow)—10% (Approx.)

Bentley in 1980—5%

The company has recently taken steps to reverse this decline of the Bentley, and three new models have appeared which are described in Chapter 31. Bentley production has risen substantially and is now approaching one-third that of Rolls-Royce. This new emphasis will undoubtedly help the prices of used post-1946 Bentleys.

We turn now to a consideration of the specific characteristics of each postwar model.

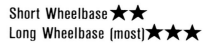

Short Wheelbase ★★
Long Wheelbase (most)★★★

History

The Silver Wraith, as the name implies, was the direct continuation of the prewar Wraith. The engine bore and stroke were the same but the design was entirely new. The block was now one piece and an F-head with overhead inlet and side exhaust valves was fitted to allow larger valve diameters. A belt drive was used for the generator and water pump. This reduced the number of gears at the front of the engine to two, from the Wraith's three and the 25/30's five. The chassis was entirely new but followed the Wraith pattern. The front springs were no longer enclosed in an oil-filled case but followed conventional independent front suspension designs with antidive characteristics, a problem on the Wraith and Phantom III. The four-wheel hydraulic jacks were gone and the wire wheels of the Wraith were replaced by conventional disc wheels. The four-wheel adjustable shocks were reduced to two on the rear only, controlled still by a hydraulic pump. The front shocks were conventional. The floor handbrake gave way to an umbrella-type pull-on unit mounted under the dashboard.

In many ways the Silver Wraith had lost the expensive idiosyncrasies of the prewar car, and it was less expensive to build. The end result, however, was still a car of great smoothness; perhaps not as dead quiet as the old Wraith, which, in turn, was generally acknowledged as the quietest Rolls-Royce of all. Yet the Silver Wraith maintained the silkiness of control and the general feel of the prewar car.

The engine was bored out ⅛ inch to 4566 cc in 1951, at chassis WOF1, and a full-flow oil filter replaced the by-pass unit. Another ⅛ inch was added to the bore in 1955 at DLW 163. This final displacement of 4887 cc was the limit of the postwar six-cylinder block. Horsepower had gone from 125 to 178. The Hydra-matic transmission was optionally offered first in 1953 at WVH1 and was standardized about 1955.

The long-wheelbase chassis of 133 inches became available in 1951 as an option and was standardized a year later. Tire size on the short-wheelbase car was 6.50x17, but the long-wheelbase car was fitted with 7.50x16's.

Power steering was available in 1956 at chassis number FLW1, a useful feature as the car gained weight. Left-hand drive first appeared in 1950 on the WGC chassis series (always denoted by an L preceding the chassis number) and was fitted with a steering-column gear change until the Hydra-matic transmission appeared. The single downdraft carburetor by Stromberg and then Zenith gave way to twin SU's in 1956.

Identification

The postwar Silver Wraith has the "proper" Rolls-Royce look when fitted with the handsome Lucas R100 headlamps. Park Ward began the move to smaller lamps in the interest of cleaner lines, but with the loss of the commanding frontal appearance. By the end of the Silver Wraith production in 1959, the big free-standing lamps were a rarity.

The larger tires on the sixteen-inch wheels are a convenient check on the long-wheelbase car and the sheer size of the later Silver Wraith sets it apart from the early short-wheelbase car which often had close-coupled coachwork. The wheel covers or nave plates changed in style about 1950, the concave plated center giving way to a new, flatter design which emphasized the plating on the rim edge.

Performance and Utility

The Silver Wraith, in all forms, is an entirely modern car and may be used readily for all purposes. Brakes and handling are to the usual high standards.

The floor shift of the early right-hand-drive cars remains exceptionally pleasant though early left-hand-drive models with the column shift are heavy to use and can have slackness. The automatic

Hooper's standard limousine, here shown on chassis number BLW22, was deservedly popular and showed Hooper's superb treatment of the rear quarter. These elegant cars have remained in service and command strong prices. Frank Dale photo.

The very early postwar Silver Wraiths were compact with strong resemblances to prewar styling. This 1947 James Young saloon is no exception. These very early cars are often low priced because they lack the majesty of the long-wheelbase cars of the fifties. Frank Dale photo.

transmission, so often maligned by purists, is well suited to the Silver Wraith and has enhanced the market value as time goes on. Likewise, the power steering is desirable on the long-wheelbase models.

The sheer bulk of the Silver Wraith, especially in long-wheelbase form, can make it a "handful" in casual use around town, but few cars have such comfortable long-range touring capabilities.

Problem Areas

Early Silver Wraiths up to chassis WCB 30 had chrome plating on the top 2¼ inches of the cylinder wall. This plating could wear away causing excessive oil consumption at relatively low milages (50,000). Beginning with chassis WCB 31, a "Bricrome" liner was fitted to this area. These liners have not proven entirely satisfactory, either, and would shrink, interrupting heat flow to the block. This resulted in overheating of the piston, broken rings and occasional piston failure. Though twin liners were offered by Rolls-Royce, "Bricrome" for the upper and cast iron for the lower parts of the cylinder wall, the best solution is a single, full-length alloy liner (Rolls-Royce part #RH 7900). Many of these early engines have been so fitted during rebuilding.

Early cars had fiber timing gears which were perishable and replaced by aluminum gears. The timing cover was then stamped with an A.

The 4½ liter engine with full-flow filter, beginning at chassis WOF 1, has proven to be a more durable unit.

The manual transmission is nearly indestructible, though first gear may become noisy. Maintenance on the automatic transmission must not be forgotten, but expensive rebuilds may be in store from time to time in any circumstances.

Always check for rust and corrosion on chassis components, especially on production from the forties when steel quality was low. It is only prudent on cars of this age to check front end bushings for looseness. Brakes are often ignored and the servo system may mask wear.

Given reasonable maintenance, the Silver Wraith is a very tough car capable of long, trouble-free service.

Coachwork

No Rolls-Royce model offered more hazards in coachwork than the Silver Wraith. Though individual designs were still executed by the various builders, batch production became the rule. Thus a particular numbered design might have ten or even 100 copies. Silver Wraiths are frequently advertised as one-off or unique designs when in truth there may be many examples of the same body in existence. It is essential to use Lawrence Dalton's *Rolls-Royce: The Elegance Continues* when shopping in this market. Dalton has substantial chassis lists for Freestone and Webb, Hooper, H. J. Mulliner and James Young against which any car can be checked, not only for batch production but for date.

A more subjective question is that of esthetics. Though initial postwar production echoed the styles of the prewar Wraith, the bodies were heavier, of larger dimensions and frequently not as pretty as earlier designs. The early Park Ward styles were among the more awkward and even the rounded lines of the saloon coachwork of the fifties have not aged gracefully. Better was the typical Hooper Teviot saloon of the early period, and the H. J. Mulliner line was even more balanced in the similar close-coupled or touring saloon. Though these evaluations remain personal, the marketplace reflects a similar appraisal.

A fundamental problem was the lack of structural support in some of the larger bodies. Heavy coachbuilt doors frequently sag and fenders and other sheet metal may become limp as structural wood decays. It is essential that door posts and wood subject to road splash be very carefully checked. Aluminum panels are not immune from corrosion and may frequently be in a bad state. Poor repair may provide temporary cosmetic sheen but cracks and wracking of body parts may quickly develop with any use.

Repair and restoration of coachbuilt bodies is exceptionally costly and must be figured against a purchase price. A "floppy" body can even require major replacement of much of the structural wood and some reskinning which may cost as much as the car itself. The decay of interior polished woodwork through moisture and abuse is equally expensive to remedy. Leather replacement may cost many thousands of dollars. The best car one can find, even at a higher price, may be the long-run bargain.

H. J. Mulliner offered this interior on the seven-passenger Silver Wraith in the early fifties. Without the jump seats, Mulliner would often provide full wood veneering on the division to the rear with the usual picnic tables and a folding foot rest below. Rolls-Royce Ltd. photo.

Freestone & Webb's four-door six-window saloon/limousine is sometimes confused with H. J. Mulliner's work. This example, WHD76, was at Earl's Court in 1950. Frank Dale photo.

Summary and Prospects

The Silver Wraith remains a car that is hard to pinpoint in terms of market prospects because it varies so much in description and coachwork. An early 1947 close-coupled Park Ward saloon in sad shape is a far cry from an immaculate 1959 H. J. Mulliner limousine with power steering and air conditioning. Condition is such a critically important factor too because many of these cars have been driven high mileages without maintenance and with the coachwork largely ignored.

One must first make an esthetic judgment and decide what pleases. A premium may be paid for the large Lucas lamps or a particular coachbuilder or an attractive style.

In general, one then evaluates the interior, looking for originality and completeness in every aspect. Such a car, of whatever body type, is more likely to have a "future." Heavily restored cars, often with incorrect materials or bizarre color choices, are without much hope. A good, honest, original Silver Wraith cannot but find future favor with collectors. Mechanical work presents the least restoration problem but, as on all Rolls-Royces, can be very expensive.

The long-wheelbase late Silver Wraiths seem to have the best prospects. Prices have become quite high on good examples because these cars offer the final statement of the classic Rolls-Royce "look" yet have entirely modern mechanical specification. The perfection of interior appointments can be awesome.

The early short-wheelbase cars have the lowest value, as a rule, with some bright exceptions. These cars may frequently offer a bargain entry price into the Rolls-Royce fraternity and may give splendid returns in utility and driving pleasure. They are easier to maintain than the prewar cars even though some refinements and features are not present. And they provide high-speed motoring beyond any small-horsepower prewar car.

The Classic Car Club of America accepts all Rolls-Royce and Bentley motorcars through 1948, which may heighten value.

Appreciation of the Silver Wraith will be modest and steady, since the collectors have already sorted out the best prospects and priced them accordingly.

SILVER WRAITH

Number produced: 1.783 (1.144 short wheelbase; 639 long wheelbase)

Original Specification: 6 cylinders, overheat inlet and side exhaust valves, 88.9 mm. x 114.3 mm. (4257 c.c.), single plate clutch, 4 speeds, brakes hydraulic front and mechanical rear with servo, suspension independent front and semi-elliptic rear, wheelbase 127, tires 6.50 x 17, price (chassis) about £1.800, bhp: 125-178.

1946/47	WTA 1-85	127' wheelbase
1946/47	WVA 1-81	
1946/47	WYA 1-87	
1947/48	WZB 1-65	
1947/48	WAB 1-65	
1947/48	WCB 1-73	
1948/50	WDC 1-101	
1948/50	WFC 1-101	
1948/50	WGC 1-101	
1950	WHD 1-101	
1950/51	WLE 1-35	
1950/51	WME 1-96	
1951	WOF 1-76	92 mm. x 114.3 mm. (4566 c.c.)
1951/52	WSG 1-76	
1952	WVH 1-116	Automatic gearbox optional
1951	ALW 1-51	Long wheelbase (133')
1952/53	BLW 1-101	
1953/54	CLW 1-43	
1954/55	DLW 1-166	95.25 mm. x 114.3 mm. (4887 c.c.) and standard gearbox, both late in series
1955/56	ELW 1-101	
1956/57	FLW 1-101	
1957	GLW 1-26	
1958	HLW 1-52	

When Hooper designers were given the freedom, they could produce beautiful personal cars. Alas, only two buyers opted for this pretty drophead, design number 8090, on chassis WCB6. Dropheads on the Silver Wraith chassis command high prices, if only for their rarity. Frank Dale photo.

The drophead or coupe was very rare on the Silver Wraith chassis. Freestone & Webb built only two of this design number 3087; this one on chassis WOF54. All such personal cars bring premium prices. Frank Dale photo.

The long-wheelbase chassis in 1951 permitted H. J. Mulliner to design a new limousine. Here is the design, number 7276, on chassis LBLW8. The smaller 16-inch wheels add to the massiveness of the design which found lasting appreciation. The value of these later long-wheelbase limousines is substantially higher than of the early cars, particularly those with power steering and automatic transmission. Paul C. Steward photo.

Here is a typical Hooper interior as displayed in a seven-passenger Silver Wraith about 1953. The burl-type woodwork was typical and favored light staining. The central vanity mirror was necessary because the rear quarter window did not permit the usual head-level cabinetry with mirrors. It was a nice place to live. Rolls-Royce Ltd. photo.

The H. J. Mulliner touring limousine was steadily developed, and by 1952 it looked like this on chassis WVH68. Seventy-five examples of this body were produced and it may be the best-balanced saloon on the short-wheelbase Silver Wraith. Interior trim and woodwork can be superb. Frank Dale photo.

If you are shown an early Hooper Silver Wraith, chances are that it will be a variation of the Teviot design. About 166 were built in three series; the first introduced in October 1946 with 107 examples, the Teviot II in September 1949 with nine examples and the Teviot III in December 1950 at Earl's Court with fifty examples. Shown above is WVH63, very near the end of production of the Teviot III, delivered in March 1953. These pretty and balanced cars were deservedly popular and prices are average. Frank Dale photo.

The later Freestone & Webb offerings were not unlike the Hooper in styling. This 1954 design, number 3171, was mounted on chassis DLW154. The flat bumpers were characteristic of Freestone & Webb. Careful check should always be made of the hingework and fit on the very massive doors which have a tendency to sag. Frank Dale photo.

Park Ward developed a refined saloon on the Silver Wraith chassis in the late fifties, of which this 1957 example is typical. Park Ward was among the earliest of the coachbuilders to adopt small head-lamps. Many collectors prefer the big Lucas R100 lamps in the Silver Wraith model, considering them more representative of the Rolls-Royce "look." Frank Dale photo.

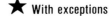 With exceptions

History

The postwar survival of the Rolls-Royce company as an automobile producer depended on new levels of volume and new economies of production. Accordingly, the Mark VI was the first factory-bodied car offered by the firm in a four-door steel saloon form, in styling not unlike the Mark V Park Ward saloons. The engine was entirely new, basically the B60 series 4¼-liter wartime engine with an F-head, similar to the unit fitted experimentally to four Mark V Corniche chassis. It was much simplified from prewar design and the block no longer rested on an aluminum crankcase but was cast in one piece. The fan belt now drove the generator and water pump. The chassis was also made available to specialist coachbuilders.

The 4½-liter engine was introduced in May 1951 with full-flow oil filter and exhaust modifications.

Identification

Early models have large center-raised wheel covers; later models have flatter wheel covers. Early by-pass filters have a bridge cap and small pipework; full-flow filters have large oil piping with a large single nut over the filter. Early Mark VI's have ten shutters in each half of the radiator. After B163 DZ there are nine shutters per half; after R Type B210 TN there are nine shutters on each side with center bar. The 4½ has twin exhaust pipes. The chassis number plate is fixed to the engine side of the firewall.

Performance and Utility

The Mark VI is a very usable car, entirely able to cope with modern traffic conditions and daily use. The engine produced about 132 bhp in 1946 and 94 mph was possible. The 4½ engine produced about 150 bhp and was capable of 102 mph. Hydraulic front brakes coupled with mechanical rears and the superb Rolls-Royce servo system made for good stopping power. The first left-hand-drive model appeared on March 28, 1949.

Problem Areas

Early Mark VI engines had the same cylinder wear problem as the Silver Wraith (see page 98). Many of these engines have been rebuilt with full-length sleeves. Failure to use the one-shot lubrication system can produce slack front suspension joints. Rust was a particularly serious problem on early production as sheet steel quality was poor. Check body supports behind the rear wheels, inner body panels, all floor panels, rocker panels and, especially, the trunk area. Though the frame is massive, an inspection for rust is suggested there too. The running gear is strong and rarely gives trouble though a noisy first gear is neither uncommon nor unreliable. Given half a chance the Mark VI will run for a very long time.

Special Coachwork

Of the 4,000 Mark VI 4¼ chassis produced, 820 were fitted with special coachwork; 179 of the 1,022 4½'s were also custom bodied. H. J. Mulliner built 301 cars, James Young 209, Park Ward 167, Freestone and Webb 103 and Hooper 61. Virtually all of these cars should be rated two stars, despite the fact that many have not survived as well as the standard steel saloons. The dropheads, very often by Park Ward, are more sought after and are rated three stars. But structural problems in the coachbuilt cars may be severe—such as heavy, sagging doors, pillar rot and decay of aluminum paneling. Restoration of deteriorated and abused coachwork can be very expensive.

Summary and Prospects

The Mark VI has long stood at the bottom of the esteem of Rolls-Royce and Bentley collectors in part because of its large production and widespread abuse by owners. Its very qualities of toughness have allowed the Mark VI to be driven to death by indifferent owners. As time goes on, the desirability of the smaller car, as compared to the S series, has tended to win for the Mark VI some new friends. The

In 1949 Park Ward was still building drophead coupes, using substantial sheet metal, from the standard steel saloons. This example on chassis B132EY still related to prewar ideas. Although the fender-mounted spare is awkward, the period charm of this car makes it valuable. Frank Dale photo.

One would usually dismiss an oddity like this 1948 Hooper saloon, B102CF, with the big Lucas lamps. However, they were factory installed to the customer's order. It is too bad that the lamps could not have been mounted lower. Frank Dale photo.

success of the Silver Dawn has brought the opportunity to own a virtually identical car, in Mark VI form, and with higher performance for far less money. The problem is to find a good one. Some Mark VI's can be bought very cheaply but restoration costs for a rusted example will be prohibitive. Even coachbuilt Mark VI's will occasionally be low priced but costs of restoration will often bring finished costs well above the market. This has tended to keep many Bentleys in a state of disrepair. A good example, however, may well present the best bargain in all of Rolls-Royce production. Long-range appreciation should eventually vindicate the quality inherent in these fine cars.

BENTLEY MARK VI

Number produced: 5,201 (4,000 4¼ Liter; 1,201 4½ Liter)

Original Specification: 6 cylinders, overhead inlet and side exhaust valves, 88.9 mm. x 114.3 mm. (4257 c.c.), single plate clutch, 4 speeds, brakes hydraulic front and mechanical rear with servo, suspension independent front and semi-elliptic rear, wheelbase 120, weight (complete car) about 4000 lb., tires 6.50 x 16, price (chassis) £1,785 (saloon) £2,345. bhp: 132.

1946/47	B 2-254 AK	4¼
1947	B 1-247 AJ	
1947	B 2-400 BH	
1947/48	B 1-401 BG	
1947/48	B 2-500 CF	
1948/49	B 1-501 CD	
1948/49	B 2-500 DA	
1948/49	B 1-501 DZ	
1949	B 2-500 EY	
1949	B 1-501 EW	
1949/50	B 2-500 FV	
1949/50	B 1-601 FU	
1950	B 1-401 GT	
1950	B 2-250 HR	
1950	B 1-251 HP	
1950/51	B 2-250 JO	
1950/51	B 1-251 JN	
1950/51	B 2-200 KM	
1951	B 1-201 KL	
1951	B 2-400 LJ	
1951	B 1-401 LH	
1951	B 2-400 MD	92.1 mm. x 114.3 mm. (4566 cc.) 4½
1951	B 1-403 MB	
1951/52	B 2-500 NZ	
1952	B 1-501 NY	
1952	B 2-300 PV	
1952	B 1-301 PU	

The James Young Clubman coupes appear from time to time, usually in Mark VI form. The very heavy doors are subject to sagging. The coupe form provided less rigidity, and body racking was sometimes evident at joints and sheet metal margins. Prices are average, with exceptions for pristine examples. Frank Dale photo.

There are a lot of these Mark VI Bentleys out there, and they can often be bought very cheaply. They are prone to rust but if a good standard steel saloon can be found it may be the best bargain of all. This example, B237LFU, has left-hand drive which enhances its value in the U.S. Frank Dale photo.

Park Ward produced 16 of these coupes on the Mark VI chassis and 14 on the R Type. This 1950 Mark VI, B181HP, is an especially nice example and commands a strong price. Paul C. Steward photo.

This MD-series standard steel saloon was the first with the 4½-liter engine. The full chromed wheel covers add sparkle but are not correct. The rear wheel spats have been removed. The lovely rear line is very evident. This car had but 50,000 miles when this picture was taken. Strother MacMinn photo.

James Young was responsible for this saloon built in 1952. It was not very pretty, and resembled the Park Ward offerings of the time. Young soon turned to crisper surface development. Frank Dale photo.

Hermann Graber in Switzerland built on the Bentley chassis. This early effort on B146MD may look better in profile. Later Graber bodies showed lower radiators and improved harmony. Frank Dale photo.

In 1951 Freestone & Webb built this very pretty coupe. If one could be found in good shape it would bring an appropriate strong price. Personal cars became rarer as the fifties moved forward. Frank Dale photo.

The Freestone & Webb saloon, an example of which is shown here on B8MD, is sometimes mistaken for the similar H. J. Mulliner saloon, but the Freestone line was more flowing and, in this case, very refined. These coachbuilt Bentleys have not survived as well as the standard steel saloons—check the doors to see if they have "fallen." Frank Dale photo.

History

The Silver Dawn was introduced in July 1949 as a detuned version of the Bentley Mark VI to broaden the market and to overcome resistance of North American buyers to the relatively unknown Bentley. Principal changes were the fitting of a Stromberg downdraft carburetor in place of the Bentley twin SU's (Zenith at number LSFC102 in 1952) and individual instruments set in small fascia openings. Early Dawns were nearly always left-hand drive for export with the awkward column shift. Left-hand-drive Dawns in the 1954-55 period are much rarer as production was tailored for British demand.

At chassis number SFC 2 the 4½-liter with full-flow filter was fitted, recognized by the large pipe at the top of the oil filter. Early engines had the by-pass filter using a bridge piece and small pipe-work.

At car SKE2 the long sweeping trunk was fitted, following the Bentley R styling. At the same time, the 1953 Hydra-matic transmission was first offered and standardized at car SMF2. On left-hand-drive cars the Hydra-matic was a great improvement over the column-shift manual gearbox, and adds to the value. Right-hand-drive purists still prefer the smooth, right-mounted floor shift of the manual box.

Identification

Most Silver Dawns have the pressed-steel body of the Bentley Mark VI. There has been some counterfeiting of the Dawn by fitting Rolls-Royce radiators to Mark VI and R Type Bentleys, so be sure to check serial numbers. Modified cars invariably have the curved Bentley top hood line which does not match the Rolls-Royce flat radiator shell. Instrument overlay decals and monogram insignias in the engine compartment may also give a counterfeit away. Bentleys always have the prefix B on serial numbers. A final check may be found on the number stamped on the frame just in front of the steering box.

Performance and Utility

The Dawn is the smallest postwar Rolls-Royce and performance is good. Top speed should be in the eighties. The car handles very well and is entirely suitable for modern motoring. All standard and some coachbuilt saloons have a sliding sunroof. A few Dawns have bench front seats. The absence of power-assisted devices increases reliability. Maintenance needs are few.

Problem Areas

The Dawn shares the body rust problems of the Mark VI and R Type Bentleys; thus, careful inspection must be made of trunk areas, fender arches, rocker panels and doorsills. Engine reliability is usually high because the six-cylinder, single-carburetor engines are unstressed. Some manual transmissions have noisy low gears which, however, continue to give service. King pin wear and other suspension looseness is possible if the centralized chassis lubricating system was not regularly used.

Special Coachwork

A very few Dawns carry coachbuilt bodies, principally Park Ward drophead coupes. Special-bodied Dawns are much sought after and should be rated three stars. Be especially alert to bogus Bentley conversions; drophead Dawns may command prices nearly double those of saloons which motivate counterfeiters.

Summary and Prospects

The Silver Dawn is a delightful Rolls-Royce and has found a loyal following. The low production of 760 units has helped to force its value up to figures perhaps twice those of comparable Bentleys. Especially valuable are cars with original interiors, still possible in the Dawn series since these cars often seem to have led sheltered lives. However, the same virtues can be found in the Bentley Mark VI and R Type at much lower prices and easier availability, providing one can find a very clean example. The higher

A very early Silver Dawn, probably dating from 1949, with the original postwar-style hubcaps. Frank Dale photo.

There were a very few drophead coupes built on the Silver Dawn chassis. This one, by Park Ward, is typical of the late design in which the front fenderline is faired into the rear fender. It was normally offered with a rear-quarter window, a "four-light" specification, which would "relieve" the vast amount of canvas behind the door. Prices will be strong for this model. Ted Reich archives.

value of the Dawn tends to make it subject to more lavish care and restoration than the Bentley. The Silver Dawn is a car that nicely combines the virtues of the prewar collectible Rolls-Royce with the utility of the later Silver Cloud I, and it will undoubtedly have a good future as an investment. Present strong prices, however, suggest an already "discovered" market with modest future price growth.

A Bentley Mark VI or R Type masquerading as a Silver Dawn should be evaluated as a Bentley with missing parts and should be avoided.

SILVER DAWN

Approximate number produced: 760

Original Specification: 6 cylinders. overhead inlet and side exhaust valves. 88.9 mm. x 114.3 mm. (4257 c.c.). single plate clutch. 4 speeds. brakes hydraulic front and mechanical rear with servo. suspension independent front and semi-elliptic rear. wheelbase 120. weight (complete car) about 4000 lb.. tires 6.50 x 16. price (saloon) about £2.500. bhp: 125-150.

1949/51	SBA 2-138	
1949/51	SCA 1-63	
1951	SDB 2-140	
1951/52	SFC 2-160	99 mm. x 114.3 mm. (4566 c.c.)
1952	SHD 2-60	
1952/53	SKE 2-50	Automatic gearbox optional
1952/53	SLE 1-51	
1953/54	SMF 2-76	Automatic gearbox standard
1953/54	SNF 1-125	
1954	SOG 2-100	
1954	SPG 1-101	
1954	SRH 2-100	
1954	STH 1-101	
1954/55	SUJ 2-130	
1954/55	SVJ 1-133	

L preceding number denotes left-hand drive.

A very late left-hand-drive Silver Dawn, LSVJ27, with twin exhausts and the low-ratio high-speed axle. This particular car had a bench front seat with a single long picnic table instead of the usual twin tables. Rear-seat passengers could eat in comfort. It spent some of its life in the Middle East and was rust free. Author photo.

History

The R Type was a development of the Mark VI with an elongated trunk and more sweeping rear lines. The Hydra-matic gearbox was first offered on chassis B16RT delivered on January 24, 1953. The few mechanical changes included an automatic choke which caused the removal of the choke and throttle controls from the steering column. Two useful changes were an increase in compression in April 1953 from 6.4 to 6.75:1 (B93TO), and a drop in the rear axle ratio from 3.727 to 3.42:1 in June 1954 (B1YA).

Identification

The longer trunk with a top-hinging lid is much larger than the bottom-opening Mark VI and the spare tire is contained in a lower compartment beneath the main trunk lid. Coachbuilt R Types are more difficult to distinguish from Mark VI's and chassis numbers should always be checked on the plate on the firewall by the engine.

Performance and Utility

The R Type standard steel saloon in high-compression form was capable of about 105 mph. It continued and refined the excellent drivability of the Mark VI. The close-ratio manual box and 3.42:1 axle made for fine high-speed driving.

Problem Areas

The R Type had a very high level of reliability with no outstanding problems. Check for rust in the steel saloons, though quality should be better than in early Mark VI's. Check radiators for sludge. Brakes are often neglected because of the superb servo system.

Special Coachwork

There were 303 R Types with custom coachwork. James Young is responsible for sixty-nine, H. J. Mulliner sixty-seven, Park Ward fifty, Hooper forty-one and Freestone and Webb twenty-nine. Harold Radford supplied his "Countryman" conversion to twenty cars while Abbott built sixteen coupes which are sometimes offered as "pre-production" Continentals, which they are not. The Swiss firm of Graber built seven bodies and Franay two, and the other two bodies are not accounted for. Many of these coachbuilt Bentley R Types were saloons, some of which were very pretty and should be rated two stars. Most sought after are the dropheads which were becoming increasingly rare and are rated three stars.

Not many of these coachbuilt bodies have the durability of the standard steel saloon and though rust may not be a critical problem in aluminum paneling, the doors may sag and the wood structure may deteriorate.

Summary and Prospects

The R Type retains all of the tough virtues of the Mark VI with additional refinements, many left-hand-drive examples and increased availability of automatic transmission. The R Type usually commands more money than the Mark VI, in part because of lower production and because it has aged less. It is closer to the Silver Dawn in price but still may often represent a great bargain. The R Type remains the last and perhaps best chance to acquire a postwar car with superb reliability linked to what is essentially a prewar style, at what is still a fair price.

At first glance, this Freestone & Webb saloon on chassis B121SP seems like a Hooper, but the flat bumpers give it away. The slight arch of the roof line is especially harmonious. The very full line of this style brings maximum challenge to structural rigidity in the door areas and careful inspection is advised. Good examples bring good prices. Frank Dale photo.

Abbott of Farnham built 16 bodies on the R Type chassis. They are sometimes *offered* as Continentals but none were actually so mounted. The line is better than many others. Frank Dale photo.

119

Harold Radford's Countryman was offered in this form in 1953 on chassis B332SR. The interior was lavishly fitted with picnic and camping gear. Radford later provided special interiors for standard saloons. Always check that a Radford body or conversion contains all specified equipment. The price for a good Radford is above average. Frank Dale photo.

A Bentley R Type standard steel saloon (B9UL) showing the enlarged trunk or boot, the late-type wheelcovers and a roof-mounted aerial. The harmonious design is evident. These fine cars can still be found at reasonable prices and a good one with little rust and rot will give much pleasure. Ted Reich photo.

James Young mounted this body on Bentley R's and Silver Dawns in 1954. It was an attractive alternative to the standard steel saloon and brings a higher price in good condition. Frank Dale photo.

The Hooper slab-side design worked well on the Bentley because the car was smaller than the Rolls-Royce. Maintaining the alignment of doors and panels was not always easy. The condition of the coachbuilt Bentleys is critical and determines price in a more acute way than on the Rolls-Royce. This is chassis number B156YD. Frank Dale photo.

BENTLEY R TYPE

Number produced: 2.320

Original Specification: same as 4½ Litre Mark VI except automatic gearbox optional. Increased overall length.

1952/53	B 2-120 RT	1953/54	B 1-251 UL
1952/53	B 1-121 RS	1953/54	B 2-250 UM
1952/53	B 2-500 SR	1953/54	B 2-300 WH
1952/53	B 1-501 SP	1954	B 1-301 WG
1953	B 1-401-TO	1954	B 2-140 XF
1953	B 2-600 TN	1954	B 1-331 YA
		1954	B 2-330 YD
		1954/55	B 1-251 ZX
		1954/55	B 2-250 ZY

History

The R Type Continental has become a "cult" car, and deservedly so. It represented the reentry of the firm into the high-speed touring market with which the Bentley marque had long been associated. Careful attention to weight and drag plus numerous modifications for high-speed cruising resulted in a car capable of nearly 120 mph, the fastest production car of its time. The very low production has enhanced the mystique of the R Continental. Stanley Sedgwick has confirmed that 169 survive, with thirty-five units still untraceable and four destroyed, so the cars have been preserved with much care.

Identification

All Continentals have a distinctive chassis number beginning with BC. Of the total production, 193 have the H. J. Mulliner fastback coupe body by which the car is normally identified. Tachometers are fitted to Continentals.

Performance and Utility

From rest through the gears to 60 mph took 13.5 seconds, and to 100 mph, 36 seconds. Top speed in first gear was 44 mph; second, 77 mph; third, 100 mph; and top, about 116 mph (at 4300 rpm in intermediate gears). There have been few cars since which can offer extremely high-speed touring with such refinement and reliability. The R Type Continental presented no mechanical complexities beyond those of the standard R series. There were 165 with right-hand drive, of which thirty-three were with automatic transmission and five with central change. Of the remaining left-hand-drive models, eleven had the steering column change, twenty-three with central floor change and nine with automatic. Purists shun the Hydra-matic because the ratios are much wider, but there are advantages (see below). Early models may be slightly faster by virtue of low weight but the D and E series with the 4887 cc engine give little away.

Problem Areas

The exceptionally high gearing of the Continental places a heavy burden upon low gear which has a ratio of only 8.222:1. In urban use, low gear often will become noisy. Likewise, the clutch is called upon for hard work in city driving and may require frequent replacement, perhaps even at 50,000-mile intervals. For this sort of regular service, the Hydra-matic transmission is probably better suited and several manual boxes were converted by owners who could not properly use the clutch. The central gear change, found on the majority of left-hand-drive cars, was not as good mechanically as the steering column shift because in both cases the linkage went to the right side of the gearbox.

Special Coachwork

All of the H. J. Mulliner coupes were superbly finished and closely identified with the Continental image. The remaining bodies were produced as follows: Franay, five; Graber, three; Farina, one; Park Ward coupe, two; and Park Ward drophead coupe, four. These bodies, by their rarity, may command premium prices—especially the dropheads.

Summary and Prospects

The R Type Continental remains one of the all-time high-speed touring motor cars and deserves a prominent place in any collection. Its continuing utility makes it a rare exception from other exotics. That a thirty-year-old car can still produce 100 mph cruising speed without undue trouble is a testimony to the greatness of this model. This car is expensive, and deservedly so, but pride of ownership and the sheer pleasure of driving will always ensure its value. The few fortunate owners of the R Type Continental may be assured of both long-term delight and steady appreciation.

Of the 208 Bentley R Type Continentals, 193 were like this H. J. Mulliner sports saloon, BC20C. The normal specification was right-hand drive with right-hand floor gear-change lever. There were, however, 43 left-hand-drive R Types built. Prices are high for this cult car. This R Type Continental is distinguished by great attention to weight reduction, which enhanced performance. The finished saloon weighed under 3,800 pounds. Beginning with the D series, the big 4.9-liter engine was fitted and when mated to a particularly light body produced brilliant performance. The S1 Continental weighed about 250 pounds more than the R, and the S2 Continental was about 450 pounds heavier than the S1. The initial character of the R Continental was thus diluted. By the time of the S3 Series, mechanical specification for the Continental was virtually identical to the standard chassis. Frank Dale photos.

BENTLEY R TYPE CONTINENTAL

Number produced: 208. bhp: 153-178.

1951/53	BC 1-26 A	R-type, weight about 3,700 lbs.
1953/54	BC 1-25 B	
1953/55	BC 1-78 C	
1954/55	BC 1-74 D	
1955	BC 1-9 E	

 With exceptions

History

The success of the Silver Dawn, the necessity of volume production for profit and the decline of independent coachbuilders made the Silver Cloud series inevitable. The Rolls-Royce and Bentley marques were drawing closer in specification and further "badge engineering" would lower unit costs. The Silver Cloud thus became the bridge by which Rolls-Royce moved from a custom coachbuilt motorcar to a standard assembly-line product. Though the Silver Wraith continued until 1959, the future policy of the company was set with the Cloud series.

The Silver Cloud body was a handsome design that combined a modified knife-edge style with voluptuous, curving fender lines. To the credit of Rolls-Royce, the American fin craze was entirely ignored, though a few of the remaining coachbuilders flirted with fins on custom bodies. Because of the conservative styling, the Silver Cloud has aged very well, though at the time of introduction, it was sometimes criticized as being too bulbous.

The 4877 cc six-cylinder engine was coupled to the Hydra-matic transmission, standard then on the Rolls-Royce. Power steering was available in March 1956. Power windows were also offered in 1959 with a complicated chain-driven system that was not entirely reliable. Interior trim and fittings were of the highest class and continued the superb level of finish that distinguished Rolls-Royce from all other cars.

Identification

The chassis plate continued to be found on the firewall. Watch out for Bentley counterfeits, which will have serial numbers preceded by a B. The Bentley side molding ends a few inches short of the radiator.

Performance and Utility

The Silver Cloud remains entirely current in terms of performance, and power-assisted steering with automatic transmission answers any questions of driving ease. The engine has extraordinary long life and with excellent maintenance may run up to 200,000 miles without a major overhaul. The new four-wheel hydraulic brakes were still servo-operated off of the transmission and are superb. The Silver Cloud I continues to give satisfaction to hundreds of owners.

Problem Areas

The mechanics of the Silver Cloud I are immensely reliable and basic troubles are infrequent. The automatic transmission may require more maintenance than the engine. The Silver Cloud I is vulnerable to leaks of the heater control diaphragms and many little hoses in the heating system, and regular inspection is essential. Power steering hoses can burst spraying flammable fluid on hot manifolds. The steel bodies rusted, sufficiently so that in 1960 the factory called attention to one particular problem in the front fender between the rear baffle plate and skin. Corrosion is also found in the rocker panels, rear trunk area, under all fenders, especially in the rear, and any place where water may be retained.

Air conditioning was fitted in the trunk by the factory about 1958, with numerous modifications such as triple fan belts, a different radiator top filler and a single matching control knob in the very center of the dash. This early system blows cold air from ducts behind the rear seat. It can still do the job (though one may need a scarf in the rear seat) but refrigerant leaking is not unlikely after thiry years.

Several add-on systems were sold in the U.S. and had under-dash controls. The factory engine modifications were often not done and these systems may be less reliable.

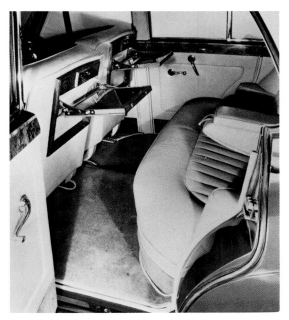

The standard interior of the Silver Cloud I and Bentley S1 was sumptuous. The hot and cold air duct may be seen on the floor behind the far seat. Picnic tables, ashtrays and vanity mirrors set in the rear quarters at head height were beautifully executed. No production car has ever been able to convey such sensual delight in seemingly ordinary interior materials. Rolls-Royce Ltd. photo.

James Young built this saloon in 1956 on chassis number SXA47. The woodwork, door latches and subtle metal shaping lift this car above the standard saloon. Frank Dale photo.

Check the power window lifts, if fitted. They can be unreliable. There is little to complain about with manual wind-up windows.

The Silver Cloud I was the last model fitted with the one-shot centralized lubrication. Failure to regularly use the system can result in particular wear of front suspension parts. Note that beginning with the F series in 1958, grease fittings were introduced at the track-rod ends and, soon after, at most points of the front suspension. Manual greasing was thus necessary even with the one-shot and this may have been overlooked.

Shock absorbers have much work to do on the Clouds, and buyers should check the softness of the front suspension. The electrically controlled rear shock firming device is very reliable.

Special Coachwork

There are few Silver Cloud I coachbuilt cars, though they are almost always charming and personal. The Silver Wraith chassis continued for limousine production. Cloud I coachbuilt cars must certainly rate three stars and the tasteful dropheads, especially the thirty-eight conservative Mulliner units, are rated four stars. The long-wheelbase Cloud I's with extra rear quarter window and with or without divider will bring a premium.

Summary and Prospects

The Cloud I has remained a favorite car for many owners because of the reliability and low maintenance costs of the six-cylinder engine. It is a good-looking car. The standard steel saloon is readily identified by the public as a "Rolls" and now that these cars are passing their third decade they have taken on an almost "vintage" aspect. They will hardly become rare—the saloon shape in all three Rolls-Royce and Bentley series through 1965 totals perhaps 13,000 units, and survival of the first series has been high. Investment potential is modest but as comfortable and usable cars, they will give much pleasure. The abundance of Bentley S1's at lower prices acts as a slight drag on an upward market. Coachbuilt Silver Cloud I's have their own market, and the dropheads, for example, have a price often double the saloons. There are few cars the age of Cloud I's which can give such elegant and modern motoring pleasure.

Once again a Bentley S Type masquerading as a Silver Cloud should be evaluated as a Bentley with missing parts and should be avoided. Many right-hand-drive Silver Clouds have been imported and are of lower value.

SILVER CLOUD

Number produced: 2,359 (2,238 short wheelbase; 121 long wheelbase)

Original Specification: 6 cylinders, overhead inlet and side exhaust valves, 92.25 mm. x 114.3 mm. (4887 c.c.), 4 speed automatic gearbox, hydraulic front and combined hydraulic and mechanical rear brakes with servo, suspension independent front and semi-elliptic rear, wheelbase 123, weight (complete car) 4370 lb., tires 8.20 x 15, price (chassis) £2,555 (saloon) £3,385, bhp: 178.

1955/56	SWA 2-250	123' wheelbase
1955/56	SXA 1-251	
1956	SYB 2-250	
1956	SZB 1-251	
1956/57	SBC 2-150	
1956/57	SCC 1-151	Power steering optional
1957/58	SDD 2-450	
1957/58	SED 1-451	
1957/58	SFE 1-501	
1957/58	SGE 2-500	
1958/59	SHF 1-249	
1958/59	SJF 2-250	
1959	SKG 1-125	
1959	SLG 2-126	
1959	SMH 1-265	
1959	SNH 2-262	
1957/58	ALC 1-26	Long wheelbase (127')
1958/59	BLC 1-51	
1959	CLC 1-47	

A 1959 long-wheelbase limousine by Park Ward on chassis LBLC47 with the characteristic rear quarter window. Such coachwork with the division brings a premium price compared to the standard steel saloon. Bob Barrymore photo.

This very pretty drophead was built in 1958 by H. J. Mulliner. Prices for Cloud I open coachwork have been very high. Photowork photo.

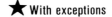 With exceptions

History

The S series Bentley and the Cloud I represented the second generation of postwar production cars. Their standard steel body was of pleasing design and aged gracefully. Though the engine dimensions were the same as the R Type Continental (4887 cc), the block was new, sturdier, with bigger valves and higher compression, to cope with the additional load of power steering. The bellhousing was heavier and the whole unit was designed especially for the automatic transmission which is the reason the very rare application of the manual box to the early S series is not so satisfactory as the R Type. The power-assisted steering was introduced as an option in March 1956 for export only on chassis B171BC and for the U.K. in October. By September 1958 all cars were so equipped.

The introduction of servo devices not only added weight but complicated the straightforward mechanics of the R Type. In the case of power steering, however, demand was heavy; fifty cars were converted to power steering upon customer demand prior to delivery, at substantial expense.

Mechanical specifications were now virtually identical to the Silver Cloud.

Identification

The chassis plate is found on the left-hand side of the firewall by the engine.

Performance and Utility

Added weight and frontal area made the S1 fractionally slower than the standard R Type, despite the 4.887-liter engine, but top speed was still in excess of 100 mph. The power steering and automatic transmission made the car very easy to drive and the braking was magnificent. The new body offered increased space and luxury and was matched by improved ride. There were few luxury cars with such distinctive trim and finish quality.

Problem Areas

The final form of the six-cylinder engine in the S1 series was immensely strong and long wearing, and was matched by the durability of the driveline components. Complication in design usually opens the way for added trouble and the S series must be watched in areas like hoses and ancillary units. Long abuse may evidence itself in the automatic transmission. The S series must be carefully examined for rust, as the new body contained numerous moisture traps. In particular, check rocker panels, door panels, front fender panels at the door openings, all rear trunk areas, fender arches and even the frame. The S series often is called upon to deliver very high mileages with virtually no maintenance because it is inexpensive and thought not worth major investment in repair. The quality of the mechanics may mask the evidence of wear to the untutored. Check interior wear as the best indication of high mileage. Also check the chassis frame in the right rear by the battery where acid may overflow.

Refer to Chapter 21 on the Silver Cloud I for further problem areas.

Special Coachwork

There are only 145 coachbuilt bodies on the 123-inch-wheelbase S1, most of which are very pretty. The rarity of such coachwork should make these cars at least rate two stars, with dropheads and especially pretty cars possibly three stars. There are only twenty-three long-wheelbase saloons with a rear quarter window, which rate two stars. Twelve long-wheelbase chassis dispatched to coachbuilders, usually for saloons or limousines built to the order of diffident buyers, are also rated two stars.

Alas, in the formal car market, diffidence is not a quality frequently found in the second buyer and the Bentley modesty is not appreciated, despite its rarity.

Summary and Prospects

The S1 standard steel saloon is offered at very low prices from time to time, indicative of the high mileage, abuse and rusting through which many of these cars have suffered. The inevitable comparison with the Cloud I has kept prices low, as status seekers prefer the Rolls-Royce version. If a clean example

The standard steel saloon has aged gracefully as this profile shows. These Bentleys are often very inexpensive, although rust must be carefully checked. Frank Dale photo.

H. J. Mulliner built this pretty special saloon on B332LEG. It is thought that only about 35 examples were produced. The later Flying Spur body has obvious affinities. Prices should be strong. Sam Shoup photo.

with a good history can be found, there may be no better buy on the Rolls-Royce and Bentley postwar markets.

The coachbuilt cars have a market of their own and must be judged individually. There can be few lovelier cars than the thirty-one H. J. Mulliner special lightweight saloons, nearly all on the S1 chassis. Bentley buyers seeking custom coachwork of the late fifties will usually prefer the Continental version whose value is less tied to a comparison with the Rolls-Royce. Thus some rare bargains may be found in the S1 standard series. The future appreciation of these cars remains limited, however, despite their virtues. The high cost of restoration and limited prospects for recovery of investment have not drawn collectors, at least in the near term.

Right-hand-drive Bentleys will have lower value.

BENTLEY S1

Number produced: 3,072 (plus 35 long wheelbase)

Original Specification: same as Silver Cloud I. bhp: 178.

1955/56	B 2-500 AN
1955/56	B 1-501 AP
1956	B 2-250 BA
1956	B 1-251 BC
1956	B 2-500 CK
1956	B 1-501 CM
1956/57	B 2-350 DB
1956/57	B 1-351 DE
1956/57	B 2-650 EG
1957/58	B 1-651 EK
1957/59	B 2-650 FA
1957/59	B 1-651 FD
1959	B 1-125 GD
1959	B 2-126 GC
1959	B 1-45 HB
1959	B 2-50 HA
1957/59	ALB 1-36 Long wheelbase (127)

This striking body was built by Hooper in 1955 and mounted on chassis B476AN. Custom coachwork was rare in the late fifties on the Bentley chassis. Pretty examples will always bring higher prices than the standard steel saloons. Frank Dale photo.

The standard steel saloon on the Bentley S1 chassis. The body is identical to that fitted on the Silver Cloud I. There were 3,072 units of this tough car built, plus another 2,359 on the Silver Cloud I chassis. Frank Dale photo.

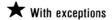 **With exceptions**

History

The six-cylinder engine was at maximum development and though top speed was excellent, the acceleration was becoming noticeably modest when compared to the American luxury competition. The addition of air conditioning further drained power. Rolls-Royce had been developing a V-8 engine for some years and introduced it in the fall of 1959. It was an aluminum unit with steel wet liners, which weighed little more than the all-iron six-cylinder engine. Displacement was up to 6230 cc (380.2 cubic inches). The new engine was easily able to handle all present and future power needs and top speed jumped to 113 mph. The axle ratio was reduced from 3.42 to 3.08, which enhanced high-speed cruising. Even with this change, fuel consumption went up.

Identification

There were no outward changes from the first series. Inside, the dashboard cappings contained new ventilation ducts.

Performance and Utility

The Cloud II's and Bentley S2's have all the torque necessary for comparison to any modern luxury car. The 0-60 mph time fell from 14.2 to 10.9 seconds, a very substantial improvement. All the virtues of the first series continued.

Problem Areas

The early V-8 engines were not entirely successful and much modification took place in the first two years. The camshaft lobes were known to wear away. The early camshaft bearings occasionally rotated, cutting off oil supply. Overtight wrist pins hastened piston scuffing. The cylinder liner seals leaked and valve guides and rocker shafts showed premature wear. A more fundamental problem occurred when the liners were withdrawn; the corroded lower block supports would tear away.

The problems were sufficiently serious that the engine was virtually redesigned, culminating in a new crankcase which began to appear in mid-1961.

Though there have been some hardy survivors of the initial engine production, many of these early units have been replaced or given major overhauls. It is imperative that the engine history of any early V-8 be carefully checked to ensure that the many factory modifications have been carried out. The rebuilding of the engines in the A, B and early C series may require heavy investment including, possibly, a new block. Happily, other areas of the car's mechanics show few problems.

The rust threat to the bodies remained but the problem was addressed more vigorously by the factory as owner experience built up and was reported. The aluminum heater matrix is located under the right front fender and is difficult and expensive to replace. Turn on the demister switch making sure the appropriate valves are open for hot water. If the windshield shows moisture or steaming, the matrix may be leaking.

The factory refrigeration unit for the air conditioning was fitted in the trunk and the factory specified that when such units were ordered tinted glass, roof insulation and silver or off-white paint must be used. This is one reason more recently added under-dash units so often are inadequate.

Special Coachwork

After 1959, only James Young, Park Ward and H. J. Mulliner were still active on any volume basis. The Harold Radford Countryman conversion was also available. Thus there were very few "custom" coach-built cars on the Cloud II and Bentley S2 chassis. As an example, there were fifty-two H. J. Mulliner drophead Cloud II's and twenty-seven James Young long-wheelbase touring limousines. There were only fifteen Mulliner Bentley S2 dropheads and but five James Young long-wheelbase limousines. Any of these custom coachwork cars should be rated two stars for closed bodies and three stars for dropheads.

Summary and Prospects

The Cloud II and Bentley S2 offer heightened performance when compared to the first series but the V-8 engine, especially in the early form, may cause expense. Appreciation potentials remain modest because availability is great and maintenance may be more costly than with the six-cylinder car. This was the first model in which Rolls-Royce production exceeded Bentley, which should have begun the notion of Bentley rarity. It has not yet worked out this way and the S2 consistently sells under the Cloud II, model for model. All of the coachbuilt cars have markets of their own and the dropheads are reaching very substantial prices.

There are rare bargains in the Silver Cloud II and, especially, the Bentley S2 series, both of which can provide much driving satisfaction. Check right-hand-drive cars carefully. They will be worth less.

The long-wheelbased chassis mounted on both the Silver Cloud and Bentley offered subtle refinements. This example, on the Silver Cloud II, has a more elaborate wood paneling with a radio speaker. The division fits neatly and closes flush to the headliner. The long-wheelbased versions normally bring a premium over the standard cars. Rolls-Royce Ltd. photo.

SILVER CLOUD II

Number produced: 2.716 (including 299 with long wheelbase)

Original Specification: 8 cylinders (V-8), overhead valves, 104.14 mm. x 91.44 mm. (6230 c.c.), 4 speed automatic gearbox, power steering, hydraulic front and combined hydraulic and mechanical rear brakes with servo, suspension independent front and semi-elliptic rear, wheelbase 123, weight (complete car) 4450 lb., tires 8.20 x 15, price (complete car) about £4.095. bhp: 185.

1959	SPA 2-326	123' wheelbase
1960	SRA 1-325	
1960	STB 2-500	
1960	SVB 1-501	
1960	SWC 2-730	Dates are earliest quoted by members
1961	SXC 1-671	
1961	SYD 2-550	
1961	SZD 1-551	
1962	SAE 1-685	
1960	LCA 1-76	Long wheelbase (127')
1961	LCB 1-101	
1961	LCC 1-101	
1962	LCD 1-25	

BENTLEY S2

Number produced: 1.865 (plus 57 long wheelbase)

Original Specification: same as Silver Cloud II. bhp: 185.

1959/60	B 1-325 AA	Short wheelbase
1959/60	B 2-326 AM	
1960	B 1-501 BR	
1960	B 2-500 BS	
1960/61	B 1-445 CT	
1960/61	B 2-756 CU	
1961/62	B 1-501 DV	
1961/62	B 2-376 DW	
1960/61	B 1-26 LBA	Long wheelbase (127)
1961/62	B 1-33 LBB	

This 1961 H. J. Mulliner has Harold Radford custom touches. The line of the car is typical of the standard drophead, and very pretty it is. The chassis is number SXC465. Bob Barrymore photo.

★★ Silver Cloud III:
★ Bentley S3:

History

The third and final series of the Cloud was well-received in the fall of 1962 in part because external styling changes gave a needed boost to sales. Horsepower was up seven percent because of a boost to 9:1 compression and larger carburetors. Minor interior changes increased room and the front seats were individually adjustable. Despite these changes, sales began to slow in late 1964 and production ceased in September 1965.

Identification

The third series is instantly identified by the 1½-inch-lower radiator which required a slightly sloping hood line. The quad headlights are a striking change.

Performance and Utility

Maximum speed was about 115 mph and 0-60 time was 10.8 seconds, fractionally better than the Cloud II. Steering effort was even lighter than the second series because power assistance was increased. Air conditioning was now very reliable and these cars continue to perform to the highest standards.

Problem Areas

The third series has an enviable service record and may well turn out to be the most trouble-free Rolls-Royce product ever built. All components were well seasoned and long production had eliminated virtually all problems, both major and minor.

Special Coachwork

There are some noteworthy coachbuilt bodies on the third series, the last chance the coachbuilders had to work with a separate chassis.

James Young produced twenty of the four-door sports saloons patterned after the H. J. Mulliner "Flying Spur" and six saloons of related style on the Cloud III, which are very pretty and should be rated three stars. These Young saloons are often mis-named Flying Spurs. In addition, Young built forty lovely touring limousines and two coupes of related line which are rated at least three stars. Seven more of these touring limousines were mounted on the S3 long-wheelbase chassis.

H. J. Mulliner continued to build its beautiful convertible based on the standard steel saloon line, but in shrinking numbers. There was only one Bentley S3 so bodied and not many Cloud III's. The combined firm of H. J. Mulliner-Park Ward continued to build each other's best designs. The brilliant Mulliner Flying Spur saloon introduced on the S1 Continental chassis was available on the Cloud III, a pretty job indeed but really better suited to the Bentley radiator. Still, all of these special designs should be rated three stars with the premium still going to the convertibles.

A slab-sided convertible had appeared on the Bentley S2 by Park Ward which was continued on the S3 and Cloud III and, though very neat, it lacked the individuality of the earlier Mulliner and Park Ward design. The slanting quad lamps and fins were a concession to contemporary trends.

Summary and Prospects

The Cloud III and Bentley S3 have found increasing favor, especially as the variety of coachwork still available gave collectors a last chance at some individuality. Prices for the convertibles have reached astonishing levels, far above the early Shadow convertibles that followed. Reliability of these cars is well known. Though high prices may dampen short-run appreciation, long-term prospects will be good. It is very possible that the third series may be the favorite of the 1955-65 production.

Right-hand-drive cars will bring substantially lower prices.

This fine H. J. Mulliner drophead coupe on the Cloud III chassis was thought dated in the mid-sixties. The market has proven otherwise and these rare cars now bring very high prices, higher than comparable early Silver Shadow convertibles. Rolls-Royce Ltd. photo.

H. J. Mulliner-Park Ward produced a slab-sided coupe and drop-head for the Silver Cloud III and Bentley S3. This profile shows the neat line, although some collectors prefer the earlier style. This car was built in 1965 on chassis number CSC141B. Frank Dale photo.

James Young preferred softer lines in this traditionally styled coupe mounted on chassis CSC31B. Styling was similar to the four-door saloon. Only six of these coupes were produced and they command a high price today. Frank Dale photo.

The standard steel saloon mounted here on the Bentley S3 is identical to the Silver Cloud III with appropriate radiator modifications and identification changes. The quad headlights are obvious though the downsloping hood (bonnet) and lower radiator should be remembered. This model, benefiting from eight years of production refinement, has a splendid service record and is highly esteemed by collectors. Rolls-Royce Ltd. photo.

Long-wheelbase saloons on the S3 are rare; this is one of 25 by Mulliner-Park Ward. Diffidence was fading and buyers opted for the Palladian-style grille. The market probably still reflects this choice. Frank Dale photo.

SILVER CLOUD III

Approximate number produced: 2.044 (plus 253 with long wheelbase)

Original Specification: 8 cylinders (V-8). overhead valves. 104.14 mm. x 91.44 mm. (6230 c.c.). 4 speed automatic gearbox. power steering. hydraulic front and combined hydraulic and mechanical rear brakes with servo. suspension independent front and semi-elliptic rear. wheelbase 123 or 127. weight (complete car) 4450 lb., tires 8.20 x 15. price (complete car) about £4.400. bhp: 200.

1962	SAZ 1-61
1962/63	SCX 1-877
1963	SDW 1-601
1963/64	SEV 1-495
1963/64	SFU 1-803
1964	SGT 1-659
1964/65	SHS 1-357
1964/65	SJR 1-623
1965	SKP 1-423
1965	CSC 1B - 141B
1965/66	CSC 1C - 19C
1962/63	CAL 1-83
1963	CBL 1-61
1963/64	CCL 1-101 (all chassis from CAL 1 are long wheelbase)
1964	CDL 1-95
1964/65	CEL 1-105
1965	CFL 1-41
1965	CGL 1-27 (Note: All Silver Cloud III numbers are ODD)

BENTLEY S3

Number produced: 1.286 (plus 32 long wheelbase)

Original Specification: same as Silver Cloud III. bhp: 200.

1962	B 2-26 AV	Short wheelbase
1962/63	B 2-828 CN	
1963	B 2-198 DF	
1963/64	B 2-530 EC	
1964	B 2-350 FG	
1964/65	B 2-200 GJ	
1965	B 2-400 HN	
1965	B 2-40 JP	
1962/64	BAL 2-30	Long wheelbase
1964/65	BBL 2-12	
1965	BCL 2-22	

The standard Silver Cloud III steel saloon is instantly identified by the quad headlights and the downsloping hood. This rugged car was the final refinement of the Cloud and has a fine service record. Good examples bring higher prices than the newer Silver Shadows. Rolls-Royce Ltd. photo.

S1 ★★★
S2 ★★
S3 ★★

History

The Continental model was continued into the S series, though with some loss of individuality. The chassis and engine were the same as the S1 but a 2.923 rear axle was fitted instead of a 3.42 and compression was 7.25 instead of 6.6. The differences between the Continental and the standard chassis were gradually eliminated over the run of the S series. Compression was equalized at 8.0:1 about June 1958; the lovely close-ratio manual gearbox was last built in March 1957; power steering was mandatory after February 1958; rear axle ratios were identical commencing with the S3. In fact, the S3 Continental no longer had any major mechanical differences from the standard chassis.

The 123-inch wheelbase of the S series was three inches longer than the R. The range of Continental bodies adapted easily to the new chassis. Though slightly heavier, performance was actually better than the R Type.

The V-8 engine duly appeared in the S2 Continental, increasing acceleration but lowering top speed from 120 to about 113 mph. This odd situation resulted from the very low numerical axle ratio which had been intended to give very high speed cruising with the six-cylinder engine. But with the V-8 the ratio was too low and the engine could not develop enough rpm for peak power. A higher numerical axle ratio was introduced at chassis BC100BY in the S3, which moved top speed up to 117 mph. It is remarkable that the old six-cylinder engine in the S1 was able to put up better top speeds than the V-8's.

The S series Continental was exported in greater volume to the United States than the R Type, especially the S2 of which ninety-two examples or forty percent of production were sold there. The S Continental is deservedly popular and made many new friends for the Bentley.

Identification

The early S Continentals often appeared with slight finning on the rear fenders. The H. J. Mulliner coupes were slightly more streamlined than the R, a bit fuller on the sides with a less-defined front fender cap line. Though the number of coachbuilders declined during the production of the S series some exceptionally fine special bodies were introduced on the Continental, such as the H. J. Mulliner Flying Spur and the later coupes by Mulliner-Park Ward and James Young. Again, the chassis plate on the firewall must be examined for precise dating.

Performance and Utility

The S series was the fastest Bentley ever cataloged up to that time and offered superb high-speed motoring. The added refinement gave it a modern flavor, but as the series progressed, mechanical individuality was lost.

Problem Areas

The S1 with the long-proven six-cylinder engine was tough and reliable. Early versions of the S2 often suffered from the teething troubles of the new V-8 engine. The S3, with problems almost entirely sorted out, was again a very reliable and long-lived car. The aluminum coachwork of all Continentals resisted decay much better than the steel of the standard saloons. Because of the generally higher prices for the Continentals, they have often received better maintenance than the standard S saloons.

Special Coachwork

There are few ugly S Continentals and the subtle changes over the production run in the offerings of Mulliner, Park Ward and James Young are a pleasure to compare. By 1965 only Young and H. J. Mulliner-Park Ward were building for the Continental. The Bentley Continental was perhaps the swan song chassis for the finest creative efforts of the specialist coachbuilders.

Park Ward built four dropheads on the R Type chassis and many more on the S1. This S1 example dates from 1958 and is typical. The R Types can be distinguished by the radiator cap which, though a dummy, unscrews. Frank Dale photo.

There are probably only six Continentals with this Hooper saloon body, which appeared in 1958. This example, BC7FM, shows the design at its best. Its rarity enhances its value; but finding one is a problem. Frank Dale photo.

Summary and Prospects

The S Continental has never gone out of popularity and the market for this car has been strong from the beginning. Mechanical restoration costs, especially on the V-8 engine, will be very expensive as high-mileage cars require rebuilding. But it seems likely that this car will continue to find a loyal following, not perhaps with the cult enthusiasm of the R Type Continental owners but certainly with deep appreciation for a very great motorcar. The fact that 1,131 Continentals were built makes them much more available to the collector at more favorable prices, especially the right-hand-drive examples, than the R Type. Careful and patient buyers will be rewarded by ownership of a blue-chip investment with much driving pleasure and modest ongoing maintenance costs.

BENTLEY S TYPE CONTINENTAL

Numbers produced: S1-431, S2-388, S3-312. bhp: 178.

1955/56	BC 1-102 AF	S1 type 7.50 x 15 or 8.00 x 15 tires
1956/57	BC 1-101 BG	
1957/58	BC 1-51 CH	
1957/59	BC 1-51 DJ	
1958-59	BC 1-51 EL	
1958/59	BC 1-51 FM	
1958/60	BC 1-31 GN	
1959/61	BC 1-151 AR	S2 type 8.00 x 15 tires
1960/61	BC 1-101 BY	
1961/62	BC 1-139 CZ	
1962/63	BC 2-174 XA	S3 type. 8.00 x 15 tires
1963/64	BC 2-100 XB	
1963/65	BC 2-202 XC	
1965	BC 2-28 XD	
1965/66	BC 2-120 XE	

Hermann Graber in Switzerland built this body on 29 Continental and normal S chassis. This one is a unique Continental, number BC25BG. The Graber design is considered to be a bit heavy but the quality is high. The line is very neat with the top down. Prices should be strong for the convertible body. Frank Dale photo.

The Mulliner Flying Spur was also built without the rear quarter window, as this handsome example, BC2FM, demonstrates. Some think it is the best-looking Continental saloon of them all. Values are strong. Frank Dale photo.

This is the well-known Flying Spur four-door saloon by H. J. Mulliner mounted on the S2 in 1960, chassis number BC91BY. It was fitted originally to the S1, and by 1964 could be purchased with a Rolls-Royce radiator shell. Frank Dale photo.

CHAPTER 26
SILVER SHADOWS APPEAR—1965

Design work for the successor to the Silver Cloud began in 1956 and the Silver Shadow was introduced in October 1965. Nine years is a long time for preparation of a new model, but Rolls-Royce worked under several constraints. The company was small by contemporary standards and the engineering staff was limited. The Rolls-Royce is unusually complex and the Shadow especially so. Furthermore, the new car was a complete break from past tradition and required very lengthy testing and development.

Rolls-Royce is a car of tradition and the Shadow, when first introduced, was criticized on the very point of its progressive innovations. The monocoque construction, revolutionary suspension and, especially, the body shape caused much comment. In retrospect the body design turned out to be exceptionally durable. When counting prototype designs, the Shadow body lasted over twenty years and showed increasing sales in its last years. This is all the more remarkable because prices were rising very rapidly. At no time in its production life did the car seem "dated" which is a tribute to the traditional Rolls-Royce goal of understatement.

After an initial settling period, the Shadow, despite its complexity, developed into a tough and reliable motorcar with performance and, especially, ride and handling far above its predecessors. The company was able to maintain quality levels of trim and finish comparable to those of the earlier days. The percentage of labor cost in any Rolls-Royce is very high, which is one reason for the very great price increases. But in truth, as prices climbed, the prewar price relationship was being reestablished. A Silver Shadow selling for about $18,000 in 1965 was only three times the cost of a Cadillac. The prewar product of 1939, in the small Wraith form, sold at a multiple of six times that of a Cadillac 61. The firm did not raise prices based on this consideration but on the factors of inflation, labor rates and the need to restore profit levels and recover capital costs. The rapid rise of prices is a particular reason why the used Shadow has retained its value over the years; the new cars with their increased costs "pull up" the used market.

The following table prepared by Robert S. Burkholder, a Rolls-Royce authority in San Francisco, illustrates the market changes:

Model	Year	Price New			
Silver Cloud III	1965	$ 17,021		May 1979	69,900
Silver Shadow	October 1965	18,000		August 1979	77,600
	December 1969	19,600		August 1980	85,300
	December 1971	24,250	Silver Spirit	March 1981	109,000
	June 1973	27,900		February 1982	111,000
	July 1975	36,250	Silver Spur	February 1982	119,000
	May 1976	38,750	Corniche	February 1982	162,500
Silver Shadow II	May 1977	48,600	Bentley Mulsanne	February 1982	110,370
	December 1977	55,900	Bentley Mulsanne L	February 1982	118,300
	October 1978	65,400	Silver Spirit	March 1983	93,000
			Corniche	March 1983	148,000
			Silver Spirit	July 1987	109,000
			Corniche	July 1987	173,800

That sales of the Rolls-Royce remained not only constant but expanded in the light of these increases is extraordinary.

Another factor in the market of the Silver Shadow era was the decline of the Bentley. In the Silver Cloud era the Bentley S had sold nearly even with the Cloud (the six-cylinder Bentley had actually outsold the Cloud I); but, after 1965 the percentage of Bentley sales fell steadily. But the fact was not unnoticed by the buying public that the used Bentley always sold for substantially less than the comparable Rolls-Royce despite virtual new price equivalence. Diffidence can count for just so much in the face of higher depreciation. Furthermore, as the prices rose very steeply the pulling power of the Bentley name faded. The percentage of Bentley sales declined to less than ten percent of Rolls-Royce production in the Shadow series and fell to five percent in 1980. Since 1965, the Bentley has thus become very much rarer than the Rolls-Royce, a factor which may someday have a market effect. (But see the revival of the Bentley after 1982 noted in Chapter 31).

The success of the Shadow was aided by another factor, namely that Rolls-Royce was the only top-grade luxury car in world production to maintain its targeted image without compromise. The Cadillac and the Lincoln were downsized in the face of the energy crises of the seventies. The need for mass production compelled such moves and with them the image was lost. A Cadillac Cimarron or a Lincoln Versailles was badge engineering in which Gresham's law took a heavy toll. Likewise, the Mercedes image, one of superb engineering and conservative styling, was not able to maintain serious competition in the 600 series. The exceedingly shrewd marketing techniques of Mercedes tapped the upper-class buyer of Cadillac and Lincoln in America, but the very success of that effort turned the Mercedes into a "mass image" product in no way competitive with Rolls-Royce. Mercedes offered a full range of diesels, sport coupes and small-engined cars which prevented the final focusing on the top luxury market. Rolls-Royce stood alone at the pinnacle of the world luxury market more than at any other time in its long and distinguished history.

History

The Silver Shadow and Bentley T, introduced in October 1965, had been in prototype form as early as 1957. The chassis was eliminated, replaced by a new unit body featuring a high-pressure hydraulic suspension leveling system not unlike that pioneered by Citroën. The hydraulic system was not used for the basic springing of the car but was only a leveling device that reacted very slowly to load, on the order of an inch a minute. When the doors were opened, the system reacted quickly for curb-side leveling at the rate of an inch in two seconds.

Hydraulic pressure was bled off for braking the four-wheel discs with a limiting valve that proportioned front and rear wheel efforts to prevent locking. The window mechanisms were electric. Power steering was by Hobourn Eaton and, later, Saginaw.

The V-8 engine appeared to be similar to that used in the Cloud III but it had new heads with the spark plugs now located above the manifolds. The new hydraulic pump was mounted in the center of the V. The engine displaced 6230 cc (380 cubic inches), which was increased in 1970 to 6750 cc (411 cubic inches). Brake horsepower went up from 200 to about 220. The Hydra-matic four-speed box was retained at first; but on export models the GM 400 three-speed torque converter box was used, with electric selector control and in 1968 it was fitted to all production cars. The big engine was mated with a 3.08:1 rear axle, a ratio used in the V-8 Clouds, which gave easy high-speed cruising.

Numerous modifications occurred. The generator was replaced by an alternator in July 1968 and the complicated front-height-control hydraulic ram system was dropped in May 1969. Optional air conditioning was made standard after May 1969. Radial ply tires were standard after August 1972. A speed-control system appeared in September 1972.

Smog modifications began to take their effect on U.S. models about 1970, and by 1975 compression was down to 7.3:1 from the original 9:1. In September 1970 a central door-locking system was fitted—with the removal of the key the transmission automatically locked itself in park position. In October 1975, Lucas electronic ignition was specified, which reduced maintenance problems.

Identification

The outline of the Silver Shadow/Bentley T was quite "square," and though it may have a slight passing resemblance to the old Peugeot 403, no car of the seventies really looked anything like it. The tumble-home on the car sides was quite vertical. The wheel arches received flares in April 1974 to accommodate the 235/70x15 HR radial ply tires.

On cars exported to North America the year can be quickly identified by the third letter on the chassis plate: A 1972, B 1973, C 1974 and so on.

Performance and Utility

The Silver Shadow and Bentley T were splendid performers and an early pre-smog version could do 0-60 in under eleven seconds. Braking was superb. In a demonstration for the author around London's Regent's Park in 1965, the Rolls-Royce driver was ecstatic about the new handling capabilities (compared to the Cloud) and he felt the Shadow to be exceptionally "light footed," as indeed it was. In August 1971 the steering ratio was reduced from 19.3 to 17.5:1, which enhanced control. Fuel economy proved to be unexceptional.

The maintenance of the Shadow is complicated and often a costly matter. The Shadow does not suffer fools gladly and expert help will be required. All Rolls-Royce repairs are expensive, regardless of model, but not every owner will easily face, for example, the recommended change of all hoses at 50,000 miles which will cost at least $2,000. The replacement of stolen hubcaps will cost $2,000. Four-figure bills for repairs and losses will hardly be irregular. Happily, the car is very reliable and beautifully made and should give long and faithful service.

James Young had but one more year of business after it made this two-door coupe in 1966. The monocoque construction of the new cars ended traditional body building. This coupe is hardly distinguishable from the H. J. Mulliner-Park Ward version; both were based on the standard saloon body. Prices are higher than for saloons. Rolls-Royce Ltd. photo.

The *Flying Lady* magazine of the Rolls-Royce Owners Club has a regular feature called "From the Shadow's Corner" containing useful service information for do-it-yourself owners.

Problem Areas

The early Shadows had numerous teething troubles, as would be expected from a totally new design of unusual complexity. Early brake pad wear and water pump failure were not uncommon. There were some cases of oil pump drive fracture which caused instant loss of oil pressure with costly damage. The Shadow was fitted with warning lights, but on early models the heat indicator sensor was set too high; when it finally went on, the engine was within danger of immediate, serious overheating. The rubber universal coupling on the upper steering column required watching.

A more fundamental weakness was in the rear suspension which was anchored to the body by a transverse box-member of sheet steel. Under abuse and/or after corrosion, the cross-member would tear away from the body, which would instantly cause the half-shaft underneath to uncouple from the trunnion. Under worse cases, the whole rear end could become detached. Though the factory eventually strengthened this lateral box-member, there are still many early production cars that may be vulnerable to this problem.

A more curious symptom suggested the devilish complexity of the hydraulic system. When the left front door was opened, the brakes could be applied and could remain dragging as the car pulled away, even with the door closed. This odd result was caused by a leaking hydraulic valve connected to the door height switch which indirectly affected the brakes. Mechanics could be forgiven for not readily diagnosing this problem! RR363 brake fluid was essential for proper performance and the use of silicon fluids was prohibited. Ventilated discs in the early seventies were a great improvement for braking.

The rubber-mounted front suspension of the early cars gave a smooth ride but could cause severe tire wear and difficulty in tracking. Any rear axle whine, fortunately rare, can be expensive.

It should be remembered that early Silver Shadows and Bentley T's can be brought up to late specifications much more easily than any other model. Maintenance history is also very important, especially in the hydraulic system.

The Silver Shadow and Bentley T were gradually debugged and reliability steadily improved. As is the case with all cars, continued production inevitably made a better product.

Special Coachwork

The unit body construction meant the end of custom coachwork in the traditional manner; but it made little difference because only James Young was still active as an independent firm. The creation of coupes and convertibles was limited to the alteration and strengthening of saloon sheet metal. The following table summarizes special coachwork.

Rolls-Royce Silver Shadow	*Years*	*Production*
Long-wheelbase saloon	Nov. 1966 - Dec. 1976	2,776
James Young two-door	Sept. 1965 - Feb. 1967	35
Mulliner-Park Ward two-door	Dec. 1965 - Sept. 1970	571
Mulliner-Park Ward convertible	Sept. 1966 - Sept. 1970	505
Bentley T		
James Young two-door	March 1966 - Feb. 1967	15
Pinin Farina two-door		1
Mulliner-Park Ward two-door	Jan. 1966 - Sept. 1970	98
Mulliner-Park Ward convertible	June 1967 - Aug. 1970	41

Summary and Prospects

The Silver Shadow market is enigmatic. It may be divided into three time periods.

A. From 1965 to 1969 the Shadow prices are lowest and many cars may be bought for under $20,000.

B. From 1970 to about 1976 there is a second market with a magnet price for a Shadow saloon of around $30,000 to $35,000. It is remarkable that year of manufacture has little effect on price. One can buy a 1977 Shadow for nearly the same price as a 1970, and exceptional examples in group A may also be found at this level.

The early instrument panel of the Silver Shadow and Bentley T was not unlike the previous models. The exquisite attention to detail was evident. Rolls-Royce Ltd. photo.

The 1967 H. J. Mulliner-Park Ward two-door. The slight "pinch" just forward of the rear wheel relieves the slab-sided body, better perhaps than the plain line of the James Young version. Perforated wheel discs were not used on the two-doors at this time and are incorrect. This car would be the last year exportable to the U.S. (apart from the "one-time" exemption). Frank Dale photo.

C. After 1977 the prices climb up to about $75,000 in yearly increments that follow somewhat the tremendous list price increases. (Distress selling of new Shadow II's occurred at about $95,000 in 1982.)

These extraordinary market conditions suggest that the prices of Shadows are exceptionally variable. There could hardly be a greater opportunity for entrepreneurs, nor could there be a greater area of hazard for novice buyers.

The development of the Silver Shadow I and Bentley T series market can be measured in another way, namely as a percentage of original price when new. From 1965 to about 1973, used Shadow saloons continued to bring more than their original list price, a result of inflation and the rapidly escalating new list price of the seventies. After 1973 until 1976, the end of the first series production, used prices seemed to hover little lower than ninety percent of new prices for any given year. The Bentley T prices are somewhat lower but the market is too small for good evaluation. Drophead coachwork seems to sell at a constant factor of 1.6 times the saloon price for any given year.

Be on guard for right-hand-drive Shadows, especially coupes and convertibles. The market for these cars has been low in England and many have been imported. Some of them may have the old four-speed Hydra-matic transmission instead of GM400 unit. Air conditioning may not have been fitted. A careful check for rust is essential. A right-hand-drive Silver Shadow should bring substantially less on the market.

The chance for general market appreciation is not clear because of the abundance of Shadows available. It is a market fed somewhat by vanity buying. Furthermore, buyers in the $70,000 region are usually capable of paying a bit more for a new Spirit. Thus, the buyer of a used Shadow should shop leisurely and spend much time following the normal market indicators. The chance for a distress sale is better with a Shadow than any other Rolls-Royce.

The Bentley market is virtually invisible, with very low initial production and exceptionally few North American examples. Rarity has not yet enhanced value.

SILVER SHADOW AND BENTLEY "T"

Number produced: Rolls-Royce saloon 16.717; Rolls-Royce long wheelbase 2.776; Bentley 1.712

Original Specification: 8 cylinders (V-8), overhead valves, 6230 cc., 4 speed automatic gearbox, power steering, hydraulic disc brakes and mechanical hand brake, suspension independent front and rear, automatic height control. Production began in 1966. bhp: 200-220.

With the Silver Shadow and Bentley "T," a completely new numbering system was started. Every chassis number has three letters followed by four digits. Since these digits are the same as the engine number, the latter have been omitted.

The following table explains the system:

First Letter	Second Letter	Third Letter
S Standard	R Rolls-Royce	H Right-hand Drive (Home)
L Long w/base	B Bentley	X Left-hand Drive (Export)
C Coachbuilt		A 1972 Left-hand drive
D Drophead (started about No. 6646)		B 1973 do
P Phantom VI		C 1974 do
		D 1975 do
		E 1976 do
J Camargue		F 1977 do
		G 1978 do
		K 1979 do

Chassis Dates

1966/67	1000 to 5999
1968/69	6000 to 8999
1970/71	9000 and up (*)

(*) if third letter is A, B, or C, see previous table.
Cars complying with U.S. safety standards start with No. 6000. Jan. 1, 1968
Silver Shadow II, Silver Wraith II and Bentley T.2 start at No. 30.000

The early Shadow dropheads have become quite popular despite prices that are often double those of the saloons. Yet good examples of the Cloud-series dropheads command higher prices. The long-term investment of the Shadow and T open coachwork seems assured. Frank Dale photos.

This 1967 Bentley T, SBH2674, is representative of the first production starting in 1965. It is identical, apart from the grille and marque labels, to the Silver Shadow. These early standard saloons have become quite inexpensive because many are available and the complexity of the design can mean high repair costs on well-used examples. Frank Dale photo.

CHAPTER 28
CORNICHE
1971-

History
In 1971, the Corniche replaced the Shadow convertible and coupe, and was offered in both body styles. The Corniche introduced several new technical ideas which were later adopted in the Shadow, including the cruise control and ventilated disc brakes. Horsepower was up because of a slightly larger exhaust-pipe diameter, different camshaft and a free-flowing air cleaner. Early Corniches had a tachometer. The car was heavier than the standard saloon but performance was improved. In 1977, the Corniche followed the Shadow II in technical specifications.

Identification
A Corniche medallion was applied to the rear deck lid beginning with car number 9770 for the coupe and 9919 for the convertible. Such a medallion has often been added to earlier cars and a check of chassis numbers is necessary to avoid deception. Wheelcovers were also changed.

Performance and Utility
The Corniche is very fast, capable of around 120 mph with 0-60 times under ten seconds. Despite its added weight, it is very responsive because the weight is concentrated more in the center of the car. Fuel economy will naturally be on the low side. Maintenance costs, when necessary, will be expensive.

Problem Areas
The Corniche is a reliable car and will share the durability of the later Shadow. By virtue of its introduction in 1971 it was spared the troubles of early production. The heavy doors can be a problem and may crack on the lock end at the slam point. Hinges should be checked. Convertible bodies are less rigid than the coupes and cross-bracing underneath may weaken because of corrosion or cracking.

Special Coachwork
The Corniche, of course, *is* the special coachwork, and variations on the coupe and convertible are virtually unknown.

Summary and Prospects
The Corniche will be much more desirable in the years ahead than the saloon Shadows. It has already shown strong market demand, especially in convertible form. The real rarities must be the Bentley Corniches—less than 100 for both closed and open bodies were produced from 1971 to 1976, or only about seventeen per year.

Collectors will surely move toward this market as time goes on. Among the Rolls-Royces, however, the pool of cars is decidedly large; greater, for example, than the total production of many prewar models in all forms! Perspectives need to be kept. But as a distinctive and pleasurable motorcar, the Corniche remains a rare treat.

The strong appreciation of the Cloud convertibles, now more expensive than early Shadow convertibles and Corniches up to about 1975, has tended to halt depreciation of all Shadow two-doors and Corniches. It could be a rare moment for a long-term investment. (See note on right-hand-drive Shadows on page 150.)

CORNICHE

Number produced: Rolls-Royce coupe 780 (1971-1976); Rolls-Royce convertible 1.233 (1971-1976); Bentley coupe 53 (1977-1982); Bentley convertible 45 (1977-1982); Rolls-Royce & Bentley coupe 326 (through December 1983); Rolls-Royce & Bentley convertible 1.361 (through December 1983).

Wheelbase: 120.5 in. Engine: V-8 6.750 cc. 412 ci. Compression: 9:1. Transmission: 3-speed automatic torque converter. Overall ratios: 1:1. 1.5:1. 2.5:1. Rear axle: 3.08:1. Tires: HR70 HR15 or 235/70 HR15. Weight: 5200 lbs. bhp: 220.

These cars are listed by chassis number only. The bodies are made by Mulliner, Park Ward. C implies fixed head. D drophead. The name comes from the famous Grande Corniche, the road high above the Mediterranean between Nice and Monte Carlo.

The Corniche was offered in saloon form but production was not continued after the introduction of the Spirit and Spur. Little has changed externally since the initial introduction in 1965. Rolls-Royce Ltd. photo.

The Corniche convertible has been little changed from its beginning in 1965 as a standard convertible. Few designs have such staying power, a tribute to the genius of Rolls-Royce. It is the only Shadow design continued after the introduction of the Spirit and Spur. Owners who bought these cars new in the sixties and seventies will be pleased to know that inflation has just about balanced depreciation. Rolls-Royce Ltd. photo.

History

Pinin Farina was assigned the task of designing a two-door personal car on the Silver Shadow "chassis." The result was the Camargue introduced in March 1975. The Camargue was a pioneering car for Rolls-Royce Motors in several ways. It introduced the split-level air-conditioning system which was later applied to the Silver Shadow II and its derivatives. Twin exhaust pipes and the new cruise-control system were offered on the Camargue. The most significant influence of this new car was in the forward placement of the radiator with faired-in headlamps which would be used in revised form in the next-generation cars, the Silver Spur and Silver Spirit. The radiator was also angled forward very slightly, a styling touch not followed in the Spur and Spirit. The later cars are fitted with the Silver Spirit rear suspension.

The instrumentation of the Camargue had a sumptuous yet utilitarian look, somewhat like aircraft gauges applied to magnificent veneers. In every aspect the interior was finished to impeccable standards.

The car weighs 5,170 pounds, substantially heavier than the Shadow or Corniche. The Pinin Farina body has full lines and suggests the mass that the weight confirms. The aerodynamics are excellent and the car is capable of very high speeds.

Identification

The Camargue is instantly recognized by the forward angle of the radiator. It is the only two-door closed body in current production.

Performance and Utility

The Camargue was designed to be the ultimate in personal transport and as such has splendid acceleration, handling and comfort. Despite its size and weight it manages to convey to the driver the feeling of agility.

Problem Areas

The Camargue has been a successful model in the Rolls-Royce range and has a good service record. There have been some brake problems with locking-on, and the height control occasionally may "act up."

Special Coachwork

The Camargue was built in the single body style with no modifications.

Summary and Prospects

The last twelve Camargues were shipped to the U.S. in early 1987, white with red interior, and with lavish equipment. The price was $175,000. With the sale of these cars, the eleven-year production of the Camargue came to a close.

The Camargue will certainly become a prime collectible in years to come because of its rarity, very high initial price and unique body style. When "big" cars are long gone, the Camargue will stand alone as the last of the truly great large cars, built without reference to cost or competition.

Prices of early Camargues have been as low as $50,000 but now are gradually moving upward. A wretched example was offered for $30,000 recently but the average price for good specimens is more like $75,000. My guess is that the depreciated used price of the last special 1987 "12" may fall to around $100,000 in a couple of years, at which point they and the whole Camargue market will slowly appreciate.

The Camargue was introduced in 1975. As a high-priced, low-production personal car, it is destined for long-range collectability. It will probably be the last big, high-performance coupe. Rolls-Royce Ltd. photo.

CAMARGUE

Number produced: 534

Wheelbase 108.5 in. Weight 5,170 pounds. Others same as Spur.
bhp: 220.

History

Design work continued on the Shadow and culminated in a set of changes sufficiently great to warrant the introduction of a new type designation in 1977, the Silver Shadow II.

Some of the features presented in the new car were rack-and-pinion steering with a ratio of 16.9:1 (down from 17.5:1), cruise control, a two-level automatic air conditioning, smaller fan with an electric booster fan, new twin exhaust system and new carburetors with slightly smaller bores but with sensing devices for temperature and fuel viscosity.

An air dam beneath the redesigned front bumper was added for high-speed stability and headlamp wipers were fitted. Both of these items were deleted from the U.S. export models.

The long-wheelbase version of the Shadow I was continued with the new mechanical specifications of the Shadow II but was given a separate model name, the Silver Wraith II. Privacy was enhanced by a smaller rear window. John Bolster pointed out in his book *Rolls-Royce Silver Shadow* that the divider could not be supplied on U.S.-bound Wraith II's because it necessitated two air-conditioning systems, the rear one displacing the fuel tank behind the rear seat. U.S. laws required that the fuel tank be located ahead of the rear crush area; thus, it could not be relocated.

Identification

The instrument panel was redesigned and the principle gauges were grouped under two large, round glass-covered dials. The fascia cap was slightly raised over these two dials. The switchbox was relocated next to the driver's door from its formal central location. The central console was much enlarged and dropped nearly to the floor.

The U.S. model was virtually identical to the first series in exterior features. The Silver Wraith II had an Everflex-covered roof.

The air dam and new bumpers instantly identified the U.K. models.

Performance and Utility

Performance levels for the second series remained above criticism. Economy was slightly improved but still in the 13 mpg range. The maintenance needs of the car were fewer than in the early series. In general, the car was even more trouble free than the late Shadow I but repairs when necessary continued to be very expensive.

The superb automatic air-conditioning system contained many subtleties which set it apart from other units, including split-level temperature control, humidity delay switches, dehumidifiers which preheated incoming air to the main system, low-pressure exhaust ducts and numerous exterior and interior sensors.

Problem Areas

The second-series Shadows, Silver Wraith II and T2 Bentley have excellent service records. The design was seasoned and strong production settled most minor problems. The rack-and-pinion steering, precise and direct, can be "sticky."

Special Coachwork

The coupes and convertibles were offered under the Corniche label, which is treated separately, as is the Camargue. Apart from the Phantom VI, the day of specialist coachbuilding had ended.

Summary and Prospects

The second-series Shadow, Bentley T and Silver Wraith II finished production in 1980. As seems always to be the case, the obsolete Rolls-Royce model takes on an aura of greater desirability as the new models appear, in part because the public becomes used to a body style. What was once condemned as radical or frivolous becomes the norm and then finally the conservative expression. All of the Shadows form a

The Bentley T2 is immediately identified in the U.K. by the front
air dam. These cars are much rarer than the comparable Shadows,
which may influence the T's future value. Rolls-Royce Ltd. photo.

large reservoir of distinctive motorcars which will no doubt take their places in years to come alongside the Silver Dawns and Silver Clouds as favorites of many.

There is some reason to believe that the boxy Shadow body has indeed already achieved a strong following and is a tasteful expression of elegance unequaled in any other contemporary motorcar. The new Spurs and Spirits do not yet have the stand-out individuality of the very upright Shadows.

Used prices for second-series cars ranged from a high of around eighty percent in 1977 to a sixty-five percent figure for the rest of the production when compared to the original new list price of any given year. Very rapid new price escalation accounts for the somewhat lower percentage of resale price as compared to the first series. Yet these figures are exceptionally strong for an automobile with such extremely high list prices.

The buying of these cars for near-term profit will be in accord with normal used-car strategies. Risks will be very high in a time of depressed economy because the Rolls-Royce and Bentley are vulnerable, especially in the used market, to a decline in speculative buying and a postponement of buying by those purchasers who have options.

It would be well to keep an eye on the used Silver Spirit prices. If late Silver Shadow prices begin to exceed those of comparable early Spirits, it will be a signal that true appreciation and perhaps collecting are beginning. This phenomenon happened with the Silver Clouds, especially the III's which now outprice early Shadow saloons.

There are very many Shadows and many splendid examples are now available with low mileage. Collectible status based on rarity will not come for a long time but really good, clean cars will slowly become harder to find. Long-term prospects should be good.

BENTLEY T2 & SILVER SHADOW II
Number produced: 8,980. bhp: 220.
SILVER WRAITH II
Number produced: 2,154. bhp: 220.

The instrument panel of the Shadow II and Bentley T2 has a raised hump over the instruments. The seat design has been given fully rolled edging and the central console has been developed and enlarged. Rolls-Royce Ltd. photo.

The Silver Wraith II was a long-wheelbase version of the Shadow. The interior division can be clearly seen. Low production and high initial cost plus interior amenities ensure that these cars fetch strong prices. Rolls-Royce Ltd. photo.

History

The new series was introduced in Europe in early October 1980, in the U.S. in 1981. It was about two inches wider and an inch lower than the Silver Shadow. The styling was fresh and was marked by a departure from the vertical side panels and angularity of the Silver Shadow. The whole car presented a slightly more bulky appearance, and the frontal treatment bore a strong resemblance to the Camargue. The interior was subtly revised, the most notable difference being the absence of the veneered door cappings. Mechanical specifications were similar to the Silver Shadow II.

The new car was offered as the short-wheelbase Silver Spirit with the parallel Bentley Mulsanne. The long-wheelbase model was called the Silver Spur with no Bentley equivalent.

Bentleys now were only five percent of production and the company decided it was time to reemphasize the Bentley by targeting a more sporting market. In 1982 the Bentley Mulsanne Turbo was offered with a Garrett AiResearch turbocharger. Then in 1984 the Bentley 8 appeared, aimed at more sporting drivers and with a slightly lower price. The Continental name was revived with the Bentley version of the Corniche convertible. Production of the four Bentley models soon increased to twenty-two percent of the total, with forty percent as the company target.

Identification

The headlights are faired into the front fenders, typical of the softening of line through the car. There is a little kick-up at the base of the rear window of the saloons. The Bentley Turbo shell is painted body color. The Bentley 8 has a distinctive mesh grille, reminiscent of the vintage Bentley radiator screens of the twenties. The wood on the instrument panel is straight-grained.

Performance and Utility

Current Rolls-Royce products continue to provide outstanding drivability coupled with many refinements that have always set these cars apart from others. Usual top speeds are in the 120 mph area. The Bentley 8 has a stiffer suspension. The Bentley Mulsanne Turbo has a 0-60 mph time of 6.7 seconds. In September 1986 a Turbo in stock form took the British National one-hour endurance record at 140.91 mph.

Problem Areas

The development of the latest series was without break in the continuity of mechanical specification and the previous high level of reliability should continue. Repairs, when necessary, will be costly.

Special Coachwork

There is no special coachwork available, though customer preferences in color and trim are always available on special order. The Corniche and identical Bentley Continental remain in production.

Summary and Prospects

The new Silver Spirit, Silver Spur and Mulsanne have been well received; however, the recession of 1982 hit the luxury market heavily. In March 1983 the price of the basic Spirit was cut seventeen percent to $93,000 and the long-wheelbase Silver Spur was reduced to $102,000. The Corniche dropped from $162,000 to $148,000. These measures were necessary not only because of economic conditions but because of the substantial drop in the value of the British pound which had shown weakness in 1983.

The Silver Spur is the long-wheelbase version of the current production. The roof is covered in Everflex. Any deviation from the normal Spirit saloon enhances its long-term value. Rolls-Royce Ltd. photo.

The 1987 fall of the dollar and other factors have forced prices upward. In the U.S. the Spirit now lists for $109,000, the Spur for $121,500, the Corniche for $173,800, the Bentley Continental for $173,200 and the Bentley 8 for $95,500. The Mulsanne Turbo may be offered in the U.S. in 1989.

Used Spirits and Spurs are rarely seen under $50,000, with the mid-range price of about $60,000 for 1980 to 1983 examples. Perfect condition and low mileage is important. By 1984 and 1985 the price climbs to around $70,000. The long-wheelbase Spur will generally command a slight premium in the used market. Bentley Mulsannes will be less. Used left-hand-drive 1984-1985 Corniches will be around $90,000 to $100,000.

SILVER SPUR

Wheelbase: 124 in.; Engine: V-8 6750 cc. 412 ci.; Compression: 9:1, U.S.A. 7.3:1. Transmission: 3-speed automatic. Overall ratios: 3.08, 4.62 and 7.7 to 1. Tires: 15x235/70. Weight: 4.950 lbs.

SILVER SPIRIT

Wheelbase: 120.5 in.; Engine: V-8 6750 cc. 412 ci. Compression: 9:1, U.S.A. 7.3:1. Transmission: 3-speed automatic. Overall ratios: 3.08, 4.62 and 7.7 to 1. Tires: 15x235/70. Weight: 5.010 lbs.

MULSANNE

Wheelbase: 120.5 in. Engine: V-8 6750 cc. 412 ci. Compression: 9:1. Transmission: 3-speed automatic. Overall ratios: 3.08, 4.62 and 7.7 to 1. Tires: 15x235/70. Weight: 4.950 lbs.

A new seventeen-digit chassis number was introduced in 1980 which may be deciphered as follows:

Digit Number

1.	S	
2.	C	Company Code
3.	A	Rolls-Royce
	B	Bentley
4.	P	Phantom VI
	Z	All Others
5.	S	Short-Wheelbase Four-Door
	L	Long-Wheelbase Division
	N	Long-Wheelbase non Division
	D.	Corniche Convertible
	J	Camargue
	M	Phantom VI Limousine
	T	Phantom VI Landaulette
6.7.8.9	0000	All cars except those for North America (all zeroes)
10.	A	1980 (Date of manufacture)
	B	1981
	C	1982
	D	1983 etc
11.	C	Built in Crewe, England
	W	All others
12.	H	Right-hand drive
	X	Left-hand drive
13.14.15.16.17.		Consecutive serial numbers for each model beginning with 1.001

Sample: SCBZN0000CCX6124 A long-wheelbase. non-division 1982 left-hand-drive Bentley. car no. 6124

(Above information from John H. Craig. Chairman and C.E.O.. Rolls-Royce Motors International. Richmond. B.C. Canada)

The Bentley Mulsanne is the companion version of the Silver Spirit; the two cars are mechanically identical. The Mulsanne Turbo is similar, but the grille shell is painted in the body color which has set a new fashion. Buyers should be warned that paint doth not necessarily a Turbo make. Rolls-Royce Ltd. photo.

Phantom IV ★★★★★
Phantom V ★★
Phantom VI ★★★

History
The Phantom IV, built for royalty and heads of state only, is the rarest of all modern Rolls-Royces. The very long 145-inch wheelbase received the finest coachwork of those builders remaining, and the results were generally spectacular. Mechanics were much like the Silver Wraith, apart from the engine, which was the straight-eight B80 series unit of 5675 cc.

Identification
The straight-eight engine and very long wheelbase instantly set these great cars apart.

Performance and Utility
As a formal car of state, both the Phantom IV's performance and utility are irrelevant. The 5½-gallon radiator suggests that slow parade work was certainly in the designers' view. Traditional mechanics, manual box and the absence of servo systems other than the famous Rolls-Royce braking system mean long, trouble-free life.

Problem Areas
The straight-eight B80 engine was very similar to the six-cylinder unit and was primarily for commercial application. It was not only tough but very long wearing. The application to limousine work meant low stress and extremely long life. All components in the car were long proven in Silver Wraith production. As a result the Phantom IV is about as trouble free as any Rolls-Royce ever produced. The only problems might appear from deterioration caused by long periods of idleness which some of these cars have experienced.

Special Coachwork
All Phantom IV's will show the very finest of each coachbuilder's art.

Summary and Prospects
Several of the Phantom IV's have found their way into private hands and appear on the market very infrequently. As a collecting curiosity they remain unusually interesting and prices will be very high. The Phantom IV is the ultimate postwar limousine and its rarity assures it of a permanent place in the Rolls-Royce pantheon.

Phantom V
History
The end of the Silver Wraith in 1959 necessitated a new, long chassis for limousine work. The Phantom V was a completely new car with a much longer wheelbase (144 inches) and the new V-8 engine of the Cloud II. The early Hydra-matic was fitted (and remained on the car long after the three-speed turbo unit was fitted into the Shadows) because the Phantom V needed the Hydra-matic's mechanical servo to operate the drum brakes. The chassis remained conventional even after the unit construction of the Silver Shadow appeared, to allow for the magnificent coachwork.

Identification
The very long wheelbase and the huge 8.90x15 tires made the Phantom V stand out even when fitted with a rare saloon body.

Performance and Utility
The Phantom V was fitted with the 6230 cc engine of around 200 bhp. However, with a chassis weight of 5,600 pounds, the car weighed well over three tons. Performance was sedate, as befits a formal car. The utility of such a giant car was limited and few owners were without chauffeurs.

The Phantom V introduced in 1960 was fitted with this body by H. J. Mulliner Park Ward in 1962. The car was well received and continued in production after 1973 as the Phantom VI. Continuity has helped prices. Frank Dale photo.

Perhaps the best of all the Phantom V limousines was the version by James Young, Design PV22, of which 92 were built. Despite the great size of this car, the superb surface development conveys minimal bulk. These cars continue to bring very high prices. Frank Dale photo.

Problem Areas

The Phantom V has had a checkered history. Many of these cars were used in formal hire work and some were ill-handled. Fleets were in both New York and Los Angeles and these cars turn up on the American market now and then. The Park Ward limousines were poor bodies with water traps everywhere and they have not survived well. By contrast, the few James Young Phantom V's were excellent. The car suffered from the early V-8 engine problems recounted in the Silver Cloud II chapter plus numerous minor faults.

Summary and Prospects

The Phantom V has not fared well in the used-car market for several reasons. Very scruffy specimens have turned up from time to time with low prices, which tends to muddy the market. The limousines are really not very pretty and in fleet service were trimmed in rather utilitarian modes. The deterioration of some of the coachwork has been extensive. All of these factors coupled with some mechanical trouble, especially in the early sixties, have kept collectors wary.

The cars are not very pleasurable to drive so that owners usually are content to be chauffered, an obstacle for many.

The Phantom V may still be bought at relatively low prices, comparable to those of the Cloud, with distress selling now and then. Future appreciation is not clear. There will always be the occasional magnificent saloon, usually by James Young, which merits the highest respect and corresponding price. By and large, however, the Phantom V has not yet found a following.

Phantom VI

History

The Phantom VI was introduced in late 1968 and was a direct evolution of the Phantom V. Mechanical specifications remained conservative. For example, the enlarged V-8 engine of 6750 cc, fitted to the Shadow in 1970 did not appear in the Phantom VI until 1978. At the same time, the GM-400 transmission was first used, which replaced the mechanical servo brake system which had been a Rolls-Royce tradition for over fifty-five years. Though the brakes followed the Shadow high-pressure system, drums were still used. Weight could exceed 6,000 pounds. The Phantom VI continues in production to special order.

Identification

The Phantom V and VI are very similar and a careful check of serial numbers is essential. The new vehicle identification system beginning in 1980 is outlined in the Silver Spirit chapter. The Phantom V rear doors opened to the front for forward entry while the Phantom VI rear doors opened to the rear for rear entry in the more usual way.

Performance and Utility

The Phantom VI has strong claim to being the finest limousine produced in the world today. The attention to detail in every aspect of the car's specification and construction is awesome. Performance is more than adequate. The utility of such a motorcar must be measured in the appreciation of the ambiance created by perfection in woods and leathers and the satisfaction of owning perhaps the last motor vehicle produced by age-old hand techniques.

Problem Areas

The earlier troubles of the Phantom V were dealt with before the Phantom VI went into production. The service record of the Phantom VI seems to be excellent.

Special Coachwork

The car is normally sold as a limousine or a full landau with top opening at the junction between front and rear doors. H. J. Mulliner-Park Ward is likely prepared to cater to the whims of clients on this highly individualistic vehicle.

Summary and Prospects

The Phantom VI is still being built and may be bought in the United States for $198,000. It is the last coachbuilt Rolls-Royce limousine designed and executed to traditional standards. Some Phantom VI's have been privately imported and may appear on the market.

There is hardly a "market" for Phantom VI's. Only one has appeared in the *Flying Lady*, in 1984, a 1972 model at $95,000. Buyers and sellers may take a long time in finding each other. If one has a reliable chauffeur and a lot of money, the Phantom VI remains the final statement of formal motoring.

This Park Ward limousine, design number 980, was first offered in 1959. Many were used in commercial service and have not aged well. Rust is likely in lower body areas and doors. Prices may be very low, reflecting poor condition and the problems of the early V-8 engine. Frank Dale photo.

PHANTOM IV

Number produced: 18

Original Specification: 8 cylinders (in line). overhead inlet and side exhaust valves. 92 mm. x 114.3 mm. (5675 c.c.). single plate clutch. 4 speeds. brakes hydraulic front and mechanical rear with servo. suspension independent front and semi-elliptic rear. wheelbase 145. tires 7.00 x 17.

4 AF 2-22	All chassis produced between 1950 and 1956	
4 BP 1-7		
4 CS 2-6		

PHANTOM V

Number produced: 832

Original Specification: 8 cylinders (V-8). overhead valves. 104.14 mm. x 91.44 mm. (6230 cc.). 4 speed automatic gearbox. hydraulic front and combined hydraulic and mechanical rear brakes with servo. suspension independent front and semi-elliptic rear. wheelbase 144. tires 8.90 x 15. price (chassis) £3.130. bhp: 200.

9/59-7/60	5 AS 1-101	
8/60-2/61	5 AT 2-100	8:1 comp. ratio
2/61-7/61	5 BV 1-101	Delco distrib.
8/61-1/62	5 BX 2-100	
11/61-11/62	5 CG 1-79	
9/62-3/64	5 VA 1-123	9:1 comp. ratio
11/63-4/64	5 VB 1-51	Lucas distrib.
4/64-10/64	5 VC 1-51	
9/64-9/65	5 VD 1-101	
9/65-3/66	5 VE 1-51	
3/66-4/68	5 VF 1-183	

PHANTOM VI

Number produced: 300 (through Dec. 1982)

Original Specification: 8 cylinders (V-8). overhead valves. 6230 cc.. 4 speed automatic gearbox. power steering. Production began in 1968.

The interior of the H. J. Mulliner-Park Ward Phantom V of the mid-sixties shows the typical Mulliner parquetry used in panel edging. The division console could be designed to the buyer's specifications, usually with decanters and glasses. Mulliner-Park Ward remained the master at limousine construction and is still able to produce interiors that convey the ultimate in that indefinable feeling of luxury. Rolls-Royce Ltd. photo.

H. J. Mulliner-Park Ward produced this seven-passenger limousine on the Phantom V chassis, design number 2003. This example, from the mid-sixties, shows the balance of the design which has remained in production, with appropriate modifications, ever since. Rolls-Royce Ltd. photo.

The interior of the James Young limousine represents the final statement of a great coachbuilding firm. Jump seats, folding foot rests, decanters, clock, picnic tables and heaters are standard items. Only the buyer's whims would determine specifications beyond these. The woodwork remains the pinnacle of James Young achievement. Rolls-Royce Ltd. photo.

James Young was very near the end of its independent company life when this magnificent limousine was constructed on the Phantom V chassis, probably in 1965. The design is not the usual PV22 but is smoother at the rear. These limousines in various forms are now acknowledged the best of the Phantom V's and bring high prices. Rolls-Royce Ltd. photo.

Very few Phantoms were fitted with formal open coachwork. Thus, such examples as 5VD83 on the Phantom V chassis are hard to find. Those with queenly tastes will respond. Frank Dale photo.

The H. J. Mulliner-Park Ward coachbuilding practices remain the same as in the prewar days. This photograph, taken about 1962, shows a Phantom V limousine followed by a Bentley S2, all being given the same attention to detail that marks great coachwork. Rolls-Royce Ltd. photo.

It is still possible to buy the finest coachbuilt limousine. The Phantom VI has imitators but no other super limousine available today is completely custom built or offers this unexcelled luxury and finish. Few were built, perhaps a dozen per year. New prices can be in the $200,000 range, depending on equipment. It is difficult to judge the market, not only because of scarcity but because the VI was introduced in 1968 and continued with few changes. Low-mileage specimens can have six-figure price tags. Rolls-Royce Ltd. photo.

Rolls-Royce and Bentley Clubs

Rolls-Royce Owners' Club, Inc.
Box 2001
New Kingstown, PA 17072-2001
The RROC was founded in 1951 and presently has about 5,500 members. Its bimonthly journal, *The Flying Lady*, is a strong publication and contains much technical information and a large classified ad section. Back issues are available. The club operates through 24 regions which have meets, rallies and other local events. Membership is required in the national club in order to join the regional clubs. Owners of both Rolls-Royce and Bentley automobiles are eligible. There are many overseas members.

Rolls-Royce Enthusiasts' Club
The Hunt House, High Street
Paulerspury
Northamptonshire
England NN12 7NA
This group was founded in 1957 and has grown to a membership of 5,500 in fifty-seven countries. Its bimonthly journal, *The Bulletin*, is a useful technical source. The club is especially experienced in organizing rallies and tours and was responsible for the Great Alpine Rally in 1973. A useful advertising supplement accompanies the journal.

The Bentley Drivers Club
16 Chearsley Road
Long Crendon, Aylesbury
Bucks, England
This is one of the oldest one-make clubs. Its *Review* is published quarterly and is filled with club news and technical material. The BDC has published numerous important studies and booklets including several fine works by one of its patrons, Stanley Sedgwick. Though the focus of the club remains with the vintage Bentley, owners of Derby and Crewe cars are welcome.

Recommended Dealers & Parts Sources

There are nearly seventy authorized Rolls-Royce dealers in the United States and many more other firms specializing in Rolls-Royce sales and services. Some of the authorized dealers actively seek to supply the market for older cars and to help the enthusiasts. Only a suggestion of such dealers is given below. The list is not meant to exclude other dealers of merit. Remember that bad cars can be bought from good dealers and good cars from bad dealers. A solid reputation helps to tip the odds in favor of the buyer.

USA

Howard Schneider
Gregg Motors
Rolls-Royce of Beverly Hills, Ltd
8833 Olympic Blvd.
Beverly Hills, CA 90211

W. F. Steward
Royal Carriage Works
35 West Virginia Ave.
Denver, CO 80209

Herman G. Albers
Albers Rolls-Royce
360 S. First St.
Zionsville, IN 46077
    A principle source of parts for all models.

Monte Shelton
Monte's Motors Company
1638 W. Burnside St.
P.O. Box 5545
Portland, OR 97228

John Belanger
Sterling Motors
445 E. Coast Highway
Newport Beach, CA 92660

Carriage House
407 E. 61st St.
New York, NY 10021

England

Frank Dale and Stepsons
120-124 King Street, Hammersmith
London W6 0RH
    The largest selection of Rolls-Royce and Bentley motorcars in Britain is on display. An excellent stocklist is published regularly.

Dan Margulies
12 Queen's Gate Place Mews
London SW7 5BQ
    Specializes in sporting cars but often has good prewar Rolls-Royces and Bentleys. (There are other dealers in this mews)

P. J. Fischer
Dyers Lane, 408 Upper Richmond Rd.
Putney, London SW 15

Porters in Kensington
11-14 Atherstone Mews, S. Kensington
London SW7 5BX

Stanley Mann
The Fruit Farm, Common Lane
Radlett, Herts WD7 8PW
    Specializes in vintage Bentleys.

P & A Wood
Great Bardfield
Braintree, Essex
    Excellent engineering reputation with very well prepared cars.

Peter Harper
Stretton House, Stretton
Cheshire, WA4 4PF
    Specializes in pre-1940 cars.

Recommended Reading

Adams, John and Roberts, Ray: *A Pride of Bentleys*. New English Library, London, 1978. A nearly full-color review of all models with generally good historical data and much technical specification. Exceptional pictures, though some of replica coachwork. Excellent value. 224 pp.

Bird, Anthony, and Ian Hallows: *The Rolls-Royce Motor Car*. B. T. Batsford Ltd., London, 1964. The best single work on Rolls-Royce. Contains history plus illustrated descriptions of all models. Chassis numbers are useful for identification and dating. 320 pp.

Bolster, John: *Rolls-Royce Silver Shadow*. Osprey, London, 1979. The first study exclusively on the post-1965 cars with much useful information. Essential for buyers in this market. 135 pp.

Brindle, Melbourne: *Twenty Silver Ghosts*. A smaller edition of the original coffee-table book published by McGraw Hill in 1971. The original is now a collector item.

Clarke, Tom: *The Rolls-Royce Wraith*. John M. Fasal, Abingdon, 1986. A full history of this model with a very useful chassis list of all cars.

Dalton, Lawrence: *Coachwork on Rolls-Royce 1906-1939*. Dalton Watson Ltd., London, 1975. A splendid pictorial review of prewar cars with essential extracts from coachbuilder's books for Freestone and Webb, Hooper, H. J. Mulliner, Park Ward, Thrupp and Maberly, Vanden Plas, and Windovers. 448 pp.

————. *Those Elegant Rolls-Royce*. Dalton Watson Ltd., London, 1967. An attractive picture book of prewar Rolls-Royces arranged by coachbuilders. 319 pp.

————. *Rolls-Royce: The Elegance Continues*. Dalton Watson Ltd., London, 1971. A companion to the above volume dealing with postwar cars from 1946 forward. Contains complete chassis numbers and dates of all coachbuilt cars by Freestone and Webb, Hooper, H. J. Mulliner, and James Young. Essential for proper identification. 264 pp.

deCampi, John Webb: *Rolls-Royce in America*. Dalton Watson Ltd., London, 1975. A splendid picture book with useful captions. Important specifications. A complete register of all American-built and American-delivered Rolls-Royces. A basic reference work essential in this market. 256 pp.

Fasal, John: *The Rolls-Royce Twenty*. Published by the author, London, 1979. A superb and exhaustive study of the Twenty with complete register of all cars, original owners and present owners when possible. Good information on the company in the twenties. Perhaps the finest book published so far on any aspect of the marque. An extraordinary achievement of a devoted enthusiast. 560 pp.

Frostick, Michael: *Bentley: Cricklewood to Crewe*. Osprey, London, 1980. Essentially a business history with substantial reprinting of various owners manuals and sales literature. 302 pp.

Gentile, Ray: *The Rolls-Royce Phantom II Continental*. Dalton Watson Ltd., London, 1980. A history of the Continental but useful as a general reference for the Phantom II. Contains a complete register of all Phantom II Continentals with original owners. 272 pp.

Green, Johnnie: *Bentley: Fifty Years of the Marque*. Dalton Watson Ltd., London, 1969. A handsome picture book of all models with intelligent captions. Brief descriptions of models. 295 pp.

Harding, Anthony (Editor): *Classic Car Profiles*. Profile Publications, Leatherhead, Surrey. England, 1965.
   No. 2 Phantom I by George Oliver
   No. 7 The Bentley 3½ and 4¼ by Geo. A. Oliver
   No. 22 The 6½ Litre Bentley by Darell Berthon
   No. 49 The 1905 3 Cylinder Rolls-Royce by George Oliver
   No. 56 The 3 Litre Bentley by Darell Berthon
   No. 91 The Rolls-Royce Silver Ghost by Anthony Bird
Concentrated and useful studies of specific models. Brief and attractive histories usually well written.

Hay, Michael: *Bentley, the Vintage Years 1919-1931*. Dalton Watson plc, London 1986.

Lloyd, Ian: *Rolls-Royce* (3 volumes). MacMillan, London, 1978. A fine general history of the company.

Morton, C. W.: *A History of Rolls-Royce Motor Cars 1903-1907*, Vol. 1. G. T. Foulis & Co., Ltd., London, 1964. The first of three volumes. An exhaustive history of all early Rolls-Royce models with some material on the Silver Ghost. A magnificent study with many illustrations. 423 pp.

Nockolds, Harold: *The Magic of a Name*. G. T. Foulis & Co., Ltd., London, 1938. An early and pleasant history. Numerous editions and reprints. 283 pp.

Oldham, W. J.: *The Rolls-Royce 40/50 hp*. G. T. Foulis, Sparkford, 1974. A narrative history of the Silver Ghost and Phantoms often using specific chassis histories for illustration. Out of print.

Rimmer, Ian W.: *Rolls-Royce and Bentley Experimental Cars*. Rolls-Royce Enthusiasts' Club, Paulerspury, 1986. A splendid study of the many experimental and prototype cars.

Robson, Graham: *Rolls-Royce Silver Cloud*. Osprey, London, 1980. The first study exclusively on the cars from 1956 to 1965. Good specification section. Important for buyers in this market. 135 pp.

Sedgwick, Stanley: *All the Prewar Bentleys—As New*. Bentley Drivers Club, 1976. A basic reference work for all prewar Bentleys listing every chassis in number and original coachwork. Critically important. 131 pp.

———. *Bentley R Type Continental*. Bentley Drivers Club, 1978. A full story of this model with a complete register of all examples with original and current owners. A basic reference work. 65 pp.

———. *Twenty Years of Crewe Bentleys, 1946-1965*. Bentley Drivers Club, 1973. Another basic and essential reference work for all buyers of cars in this period. 52 pp.

———. *Where Have all the Blowers Gone?* Bentley Drivers Club. A register of the fifty blower Bentleys with additional technical information. 20 pp.

Shoup, C. S.: *Rolls-Royce Fact And Legend*. Rolls-Royce Owners Club, 1971, 1979. A concise historic summary. Good bibliography. 50 pp.

Soutter, Arthur: *The American Rolls-Royce*. Mowbray, Providence, RI, 1976. A superb history of the Springfield Rolls-Royce plant. With much technical information on the American Silver Ghost and Phantom I. 239 pp.

Tubbs, D. B.: *The Rolls-Royce Phantoms*. Hamish Hamilton Ltd., London, 1964. A handsome brief summary with good pictures, chassis numbers, and a most attractive format. 64 pp.

Ullyett, Kenneth: *The Book of the Silver Ghost*. Motorbooks International, Osceola, WI, 1977 (reprint). Brief history. Thirty-two fine black and white plates and a complete reprint of the first 1907 Ghost instruction manual.

———. *The Book of the Phantoms*. Max Parrish & Co., Ltd., London, 1964. Companion to the above with 32 plates. Almost complete facsimile of 1925 Phantom I handbook, extractions from Phantom II handbook, facsimile of Phantom III handbook, a selection of pages from Phantom IV handbook, and some pages from Phantom V handbook.